AN EXPLANATION

THE aim and object of this book is to teach rapid, easily executed business writing. Nothing else. This little book has not been written to exploit any penman's skill as a pen artist. Its aim is to be of use to those who are ambitious to become good, practical business writers. The lessons it contains are not experimental, but in a different form they have been the means of guiding thousands of young men and women to a good business style of writing.

As will be seen at a glance, the Palmer Method of Business Writing has nothing in common with the slant and vertical copybooks that have been so largely used in public schools for more than a quarter of a century. If they are right, this book is wrong. The two methods of teaching writing are absolutely antagonistic.

In teaching writing, as in other things, the final result should be the criterion.

The copybook has but one purpose, *absolute mechanical accuracy*. The copybook headline is first carefully penciled by a skilled penman after an agreed model, and shows none of the individuality of the penman employed in its construction. The penciled copy is given to a skilled script engraver who engraves it by hand, and further perfects it wherever possible.

This impossible and lifeless ideal, the child is required to imitate through long dreary pages of perfunctory copying. What wonder that he fails!

It has been proved through at least two generations, that the copybook kills individuality and makes freedom of movement impossible. It compels slow finger action in the formation of letters, giving a fair degree of accuracy where slow writing only is required; but it inevitably becomes scribbling when the least speed is attempted. In the Palmer Method freedom of movement is made fundamental, and through a constantly repeated series of rapid drills the application of movement becomes a fixed habit of the learner. Under this plan the student's first attempt is naturally crude, but every drill that is practiced in strict accord with the printed instructions tends to add grace and accuracy to the student's work. The inevitable result is a handwriting that embodies the three utilitarian essentials—legibility, rapidity, and ease in execution.

The drills and copies given in this book are *actual writing*, executed with a rapid, easy, muscular movement, and then photo-engraved, thus retaining the individuality of the writer.

Students practicing from these lessons will acquire the general style of the copies, but at the same time there is left them the possibility of developing their own individuality.

The result sought in the Palmer Method of Business Writing, is to aid students to become what the world of business and affairs is calling for—easy and rapid writers of plain business penmanship.

TO THE TEACHER

WHILE the lessons given in the Palmer Method of Business Writing are self-teaching in the fullest sense, the teacher under whom the system is used will not be relieved of the responsibility of supervision. Supervision, however, will consist mainly in seeing that students practice the lessons strictly in accordance with the instructions.

"Practice makes perfect," is an old adage, and is applicable to almost everything in life that we undertake. In penmanship we must add, "When we know *how* to practice." Penmanship practice to be effective must be in the right direction, and hence the importance of observing closely such rules and suggestions as are given in this book.

The first thing of importance is to see that all students sit in easy, natural positions that will allow the freest use of the muscles of the right arm, as fully explained in the opening lessons. Another important matter is to see that the drills are practiced at the rate of speed indicated, and not slowly. Unless this is done, there will be a tendency to use more or less finger movement in executing the drills, thus defeating their main object, that of breaking up the finger movement habit.

Teachers should encourage their students to use muscular movement in all their writing as soon as possible. Muscular and finger movements are so mutually antagonistic, that both cannot be successfully used. The constant use of one increases the difficulty of using the other, hence the importance of substituting the muscular for the finger movement at the outset, no matter how erratic the writing may be for a week or two thereafter.

All teachers who use this book are freely invited to write to the author, whenever they may feel that he can aid them in any way to make their work more successful.

TO THE STUDENT

IN the following lessons you will find instructions, which, if followed in your penmanship practice, will enable you to develop an easy, rapid style of writing that will be a source of pleasure and profit to you throughout your life.

The special requirement is that you shall do your part faithfully and earnestly, mastering the details of each lesson, and studying and applying all instructions given. Neglect one detail, and your success will fall short of what it should be. Give thoughtful, earnest attention to all the detailed instructions; practice faithfully and you will be surprised and delighted with the advancement you will make.

At first there may be a tendency to discouragement, on account of inability to control the movement well enough to make good forms, but there must be a beginning to all success, however great, and you cannot expect to free yourself from the habit of a cramped finger movement of years' standing and develop an accurate, free muscular movement all at once and without constantly repeated effort. Do your part and the results will take care of themselves, and sooner than you realize you will be on the sure way to become a good business penman.

LESSON 1

BREAKING UP FINGER MOVEMENT

BEFORE attempting to do any work in the line of penmanship development, we must thoroughly understand the task set before us. Nearly all who follow these lessons will be more accustomed to finger, than muscular movement. The first step toward a good style of muscular movement writing, is the breaking up of the finger movement. You cannot and must not expect to write a very regular hand while changing from the finger to a freer movement, but do not let that discourage you. It is unlikely that you can write as well at first with the muscular as you have been writing with the finger movement.

Business demands a style of writing that embodies three things only: First, legibility; second, rapidity; and third, ease in execution. Legibility is, of course, of the utmost importance. Writing to be of any use whatever must be legible; and writing to be of much use in business offices must be done at a high rate of speed. To preserve life and health where much writing is to be done, ease in execution is an absolute necessity; while to the one who writes but an occasional letter, the ability to write rapidly, easily and well is ample compensation for the expenditure of a little effort in learning.

NO. 1. A VERY POOR POSITION.

The copybook finger movement style of writing meets only the first requirement—legibility. Where this style of writing is done slowly and in small quantities, it is possible to make it absolutely legible. The three essentials, legibility, rapidity and ease in execution, can only be harmonized through the development of the right application of a light, elastic, quick muscular movement. In this movement the large, powerful, and practically tireless muscles of the arm are brought into use, thus relieving the strain that would otherwise be placed upon the small, delicate muscles of the fingers.

At the outset you must fully realize the value of a good business hand, and you must further understand the fact that you cannot secure this necessary accomplishment without effort on your part. You cannot take it in through a method of absorption. It is earnest work that will count in this as in other things. There is no such thing as failure in this work where a student has one good eye, one sound hand, and the reasonable use of other faculties and is willing to work.

REMEMBER THE INSTRUCTIONS

It is of the utmost importance that the instructions in relation to general position at the desk, position of the hand, fingers, etc., and, in fact, everything affecting the writing, should be remembered. One of the greatest difficulties encountered by teachers of practical writing, is their inability to properly impress upon students the importance of remembering all of the little things. In your finger movement writing you have been accustomed to lean forward upon the desk, forming an acute angle at the right elbow, drawing the right arm down toward the side, resting on the side of the hand and on the wrist, and, in fact, assuming in the writing that you do, a position that precludes the possibility of easy muscular action. All this must change, or failure is inevitable.

HEIGHT OF TABLE OR DESK

No one can write easily at a table so low that it is necessary to throw the entire body forward to reach the writing. On the other hand, it would be fully as difficult to acquire a good movement at a desk or table so high that when sitting in an upright position with the right forearm resting on the table, the shoulder is thrown upward and out of its natural position.

It is not expected that this matter can be regulated with entire satisfaction in school rooms where the desks are of a uniform height and the pupils of many sizes, but wherever possible the desks should be adjusted to conform to the varying height of pupils.

NO. 2. A GOOD POSITION NO. 3. A BAD POSITION

WRITING MATERIALS

Do not attempt to practice penmanship with poor paper, poor pens, or poor ink. Good material is an absolute necessity. Do not use a metal finished penholder. A rubber finished "Crown," and cork finished "Bank," are among the best penholders made. Never use an oblique penholder in business writing. It is out of place and of no advantage whatever. There is nothing that equals an oblique holder for ornamental writing, but there its utility ends. Use paper of generous size for your practice, a medium coarse pen and good blue-black writing fluid.

CLOTHING FOR THE RIGHT FOREARM

As the movement taught is one in which the muscles of the right forearm play an important part, it is highly essential that these muscles should be so clothed as to permit, at all times, unrestricted action. Many good writers consider this of sufficient importance to lead them to cut off the right undersleeve at the elbow.

OBJECT LESSONS IN POSITION

The accompanying illustration (No. 4) shows a bad position. Study the lower limbs, study the position of head and neck, and then examine minutely the position of the arms. The student who persists in the attempt to learn good writing in such a position is as sure to fail as night is to follow day. Failure is indicated in every outline, as only a cramped finger movement is possible in such a contorted position.

NO. 4. A BAD POSITION

NO. 5. A GOOD POSITION

NO. 6. FINGER STUDY

NO. 7. FINGER AND RELATIVE POSITION STUDY

MORE POSITIONS FOR STUDY

The young man in the front seat (page 6) is in a good position. He can drive the pen forward to success through the easy action of the muscles of the arm, but the young man in the back seat will meet only failure unless he follows the good example before him.

DEFINITIONS OF MOVEMENT

The muscular movement, as applied to writing, is the movement of the muscles of the arm from the shoulder to the wrist, while keeping the larger part of the arm forward of the elbow on the desk, the fingers not being held rigidly, but remaining passive, and not being extended or contracted in the formation of any of the capitals or any of the small letters, except the upper loops, when there may be a slight extension and contraction in making the turn at the top. In this movement the propelling power is located behind the elbow in the upper muscles of the arm.

Examine your right arm. Notice the increasing size from the wrist to the elbow. Grasp the right arm with the left hand just below, but near the elbow. Note particularly the elasticity of the muscles; move the flesh on the right arm forward and backward with the left hand. On the development of the elasticity of that muscle depends your success in learning a good style of business writing. You are urged to read the above a number of times. It is important.

HOW TO DEVELOP MUSCULAR ACTION

Throw your right arm on the desk and close the fingers of the right hand tight. (See accompanying cut). See how far you can move the hand forward and backward without slipping the sleeve or without any motion of the wrist or fingers. The fingers must be closed so that you cannot extend or contract them.

NO. 8. NATURAL POSITION OF PENHOLDER

NO. 9. NATURAL POSITION OF HAND

Can you move that hand through space a sufficient distance to execute any capital you will ever have to make? Could you make a capital through two or three lines of the paper, two or three times as large as used, without any action of the fingers?

When you grasp the pen there is a tendency to get down close to the work and to cramp the muscles. Don't do it; overcome the tendency; pull yourself away from the desk with a mighty effort, and remember that you will fail unless you observe closely what has been told you about position at desk.

The purpose of illustrations 6 and 7 is to show the natural positions of the fingers that should be maintained in writing. Throw your arms on the desk in natural positions, such as you would take if you were simply resting and not contemplating using a pen; turn the palms of the hands upward, as shown in cut 6, and study the position of the fingers. Now turn the palms downward and raise both arms from the table, as shown in cut 7, the left hand being a little in advance of the right; drop both arms to the table and you will be in a good writing position. But let us go farther.

Study closely the position of the right hand in illustration 8. Note the fact that the fingers have not been changed from numbers 6 and 7 beyond what was necessary to hold the penholder firmly. The penholder rests against the side of the second finger, at the root of the nail; the first finger rests on the upper part of the holder, and the thumb rests against the side of the holder at the lower joint of the first finger. Notice further the relative position of every part of the holder with the hand. Now pass on to illustration 9. Here we have a good position for executing writing rapidly and easily on the regular slant. The right arm is thrown well out from the side and a right angle (turn) is formed at the elbow; the third and fourth fingers are thrown well under the hand, forming a moveable rest; the side of the hand and wrist, while near the paper, do not touch it; the penholder points a little to the right of the right shoulder; the left hand is at the upper left corner of the paper, keeping it in position; the body, while bending slightly at the hips, is self-supporting, and the large muscles of the forearm rest on the desk, the fulcrum or main rest being just forward of the elbow. Before going any further, experiment with position. Move the hand forward and backward, right and left, round and round, without extending or contracting the fingers holding the pen and with the pen raised from the paper.

LESSON 2

Wait; do not be impatient to make ink marks on the paper. That your effort may not be uselessly expended, learn *how* to practice first. Review the study of lesson one, beginning with "Object Lessons in Position," page 7.

DRILL 1

The fact that speed is an important factor in business writing, has been emphasized. In your first movement drills, number 1, an effort should be made to use a light, rapid motion.

In the first part of drill 1, the down strokes should be as nearly straight as possible and the up strokes should be curved a very little; just enough to carry a downward line to the right of the one preceding it. It will be seen that the pen remains on the paper from the beginning to the ending stroke of each exercise. If the lines run together, no harm will be done.

In the first part of the drill and in the large ovals 200 downward lines should be made to the minute, 400 combined upward and downward lines, and in the horizontal straight line exercise 180 strokes to the right, or 360 lines to the minute. In the traced oval exercise the pen should move over the same course ten times, before being lifted.

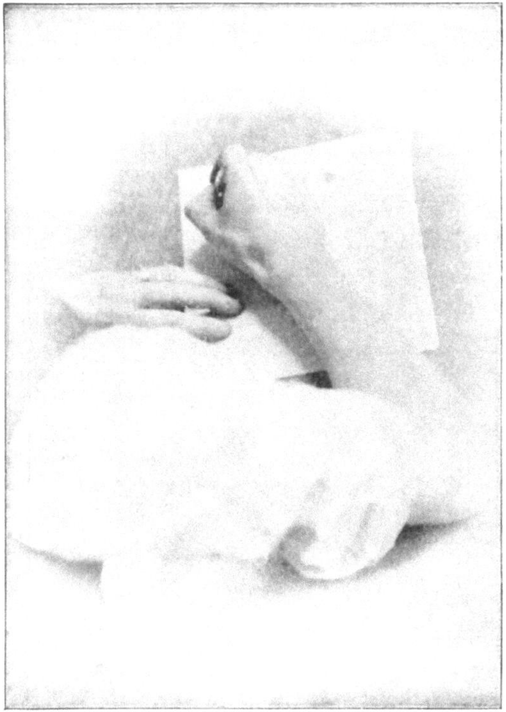

STUDY RELATIVE POSITION OF RIGHT FOREARM TO PAPER

COUNTING TO REGULATE MOTION

In developing light, uniform motion in class penmanship practice, counting is an important factor. It makes the work more interesting than it would otherwise be, tones down the movement of the naturally nervous pupils, acts as a constant spur to the habitually slow boy or girl, and keeps the indolent student busy. In the oblique straight line and oval exercises given in drill 1 the downward strokes only should be counted, and in the horizontal straight line exercise the right strokes should be counted. The other parts of the drills being what are termed connective lines are not counted. For the oblique straight line part of the drill count one, one, one, one, and repeat until about twenty downward strokes have been made; in the horizontal straight line drill the same count should be employed, and in the traced ovals the count should be 1, 2, 3, 4, 5, 6, 7, 8, 9, 10 for each completed oval.

LESSON 3

This lesson should be a review of lesson 2, and in classes of very young pupils it may be an advantage to spend an entire week on the first two lessons. Teachers should guard against too rapid advancement from one lesson to another. Each lesson is important, and should be mastered to a degree possible with beginners before a new lesson is studied and practiced. Where the classes are small and teachers have time to watch the pupils individually, it is often well to hold back for review some who are indolent or indifferent, while those who have done the work assigned in a satisfactory manner are advanced.

LESSON 4

Preparatory to the drills given in this lesson, you are advised to study closely the illustration on page 11. Its aim is to show the position of the right forearm in its relation to the paper.

This illustration indicates clearly that the author of these lessons does not recommend a position of the right forearm parallel to the edge of the paper, but teaches an oblique position of the arm. This is a departure from old conventional lines, but as those who advocate the parallel position do not use it in business writing, it can be clearly seen that in recommending it authors have been guided by custom rather than utility.

In the position shown in the illustration, it is usually best to turn the hand to the right until the penholder points about three inches to the right of the shoulder. This position gives a side sweep, instead of forcing the motion directly back against the elbow, and enables the writer to constantly see the points of the pen without changing the position of the body or head.

DRILL 2

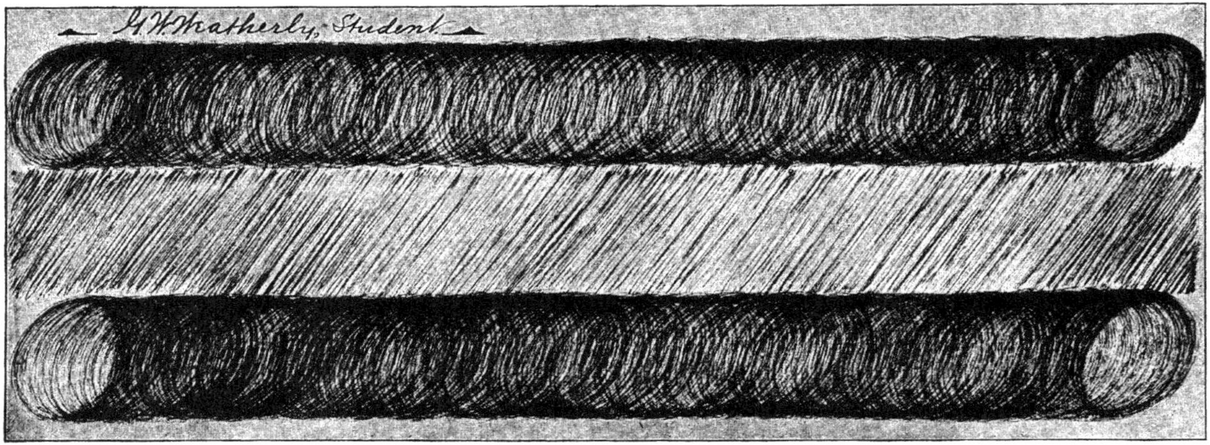

In drill 2 we have the direct oval and straight line forward and backward movements, the mastery of which is necessary at the outset. For several weeks these drills should be practiced from five to ten minutes at the beginning of each practice period, and thereafter they should be frequently reviewed.

The movement used must be very light and very quick, fully 200 downward strokes being made to the minute; and in the development of that movement we are led to discuss preparatory motion.

PREPARATORY MOTION

Read the following carefully until thoroughly understood. It is of especial interest to beginners. Before making the oval drill or attempting any part of it, move the pen in the air and move it rapidly over the path of the first oval a number of times. While doing this, watch closely the movement of the muscles of the arm, studying the motion and its application. While the pen is moving rapidly, and without checking its motion, let it strike the paper. The force thus gathered will compel light, quick action, will break up finger motion, will give smooth lines, and will aid form building.

CAUTION: Before attempting the large oval drill, be sure that all the conditions are favorable. Not much can be accomplished unless the rules in regard to position of body, arm, wrist and fingers are closely observed. Re-read the beginning lesson if necessary. Do not waste time by attempting to do something you do not understand. Work intelligently, and satisfactory results are sure to follow.

LESSON 5

Give some thought to preparation each time you sit down to write, until you become accustomed to a good position. Open this lesson with a short review of drill 2 in lesson 4. Practice the straight line exercise a few minutes with a light motion.

Count one, one, one, down, down, light, light, light, etc., the count being given to every downward stroke. Criticism may be given by the teacher in the following manner while the count is continued: Lighter, lighter, lighter, closer, closer, closer, down, down, down, one, one, one, smaller, smaller, smaller, etc. Change to the oval and drill a few minutes, continuing the same light, quick motion.

ABOUT SLANT

Slant will take care of itself, if the right position is maintained. It must be seen that the relative position of forearm and paper has much to do with slant. The photographic view given in lesson 2 shows a good position. Maintaining this position in all writing and making the downward strokes always toward a point central between the eyes, will establish a medium slant, such as is taught by nearly all teachers of practical writing. The following line shows a variety in slant, due to changing the directions of the movement without in any way changing the relative positions of paper, arm and body.

Pupils, why do we devote so much time to the development of these compact and open oval drills? Eventually, if you enter the employ of a business man to keep his books, he will not ask you whether or not you can make nice compact ovals, but he will wish to see your writing, and the better hand you write, the better will be your chance for promotion. These oval and other movement drills are simply a means to an end, and it is difficult to reach the desired end without the means. Devote your spare time to these drills until you can make them well, and the succeeding steps in the course will be made easier thereby.

The direct oval drills may be arranged in many different forms. Number 3 has been a favorite in the author's classes. First we have a line of the compact oval double size, then what we term the retraced oval, followed by the compact and open oval, regular size.

Beginners can profitably devote several hours to careful, conscientious work on these ovals at the very beginning of muscular development.

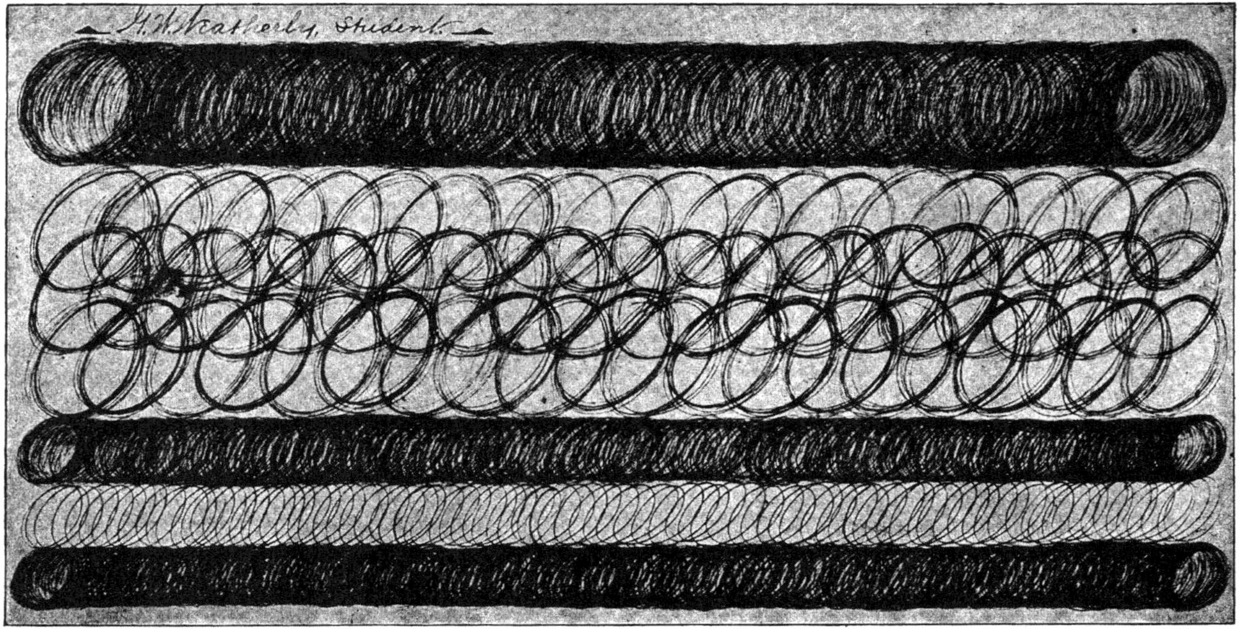

Study the copy closely before attempting to imitate it. First fix the form in the mind and then study the application of the movement to it. Use the following method of making the interlaced oval part of drill 3. First make traced ovals of ten revolutions each across the page as in the traced ovals in drill 1, and then other ovals on the same line, cutting the first ovals in the center. The second and third lines are duplicates of the first, but the upper half of each oval after the first row reaches to the center of the ovals above it.

In all of this oval practice the speed of 200 downward strokes to the minute should be maintained. Do not cramp the muscles of the arm. Strike out boldly with all the assurance at your command, even though the results may, at first, be far from satisfactory.

LESSON 6

FOR STUDY

Students will now begin to make a practical application of the direct oval practiced in the preceding lessons. The capital A of above form is one of the easiest direct oval letters. Study the constructive lines carefully.

DRILL 4

In drill 4 the special object sought is to develop a uniform, continuous motion. Preparatory to the first oval the movement should be tested by carrying the pen rapidly in the air, the arm resting and the hand in a good writing position. Without checking the motion the pen should be brought to the paper, thus forcing the pen to make sharp clear lines. In passing from one oval to the following, the pen should be lifted from the paper at the base line without checking the motion, should swing below the base line to the right and to the beginning line of the next oval, a uniform speed being maintained throughout. Thus the pen is in constant motion and no shaky lines are possible.

Students should study the above instructions in connection with the oval practice until fully understood. *These instructions are important, having a direct bearing upon all capital letter practice.*

DRILL 5

Drill 5 is what we term a forcing movement drill, and it is one of the best for the beginner to practice.

In the direct traced oval make six revolutions in a count of 1, 2, 3, 4, 5, 6, lifting the pen on the base line on the sixth count without checking the motion, swinging it in the air to the beginning stroke of capital A. Thus the student will be forced from a slow, lagging movement to a motion that is elastic and rapid. The form may not be entirely satisfactory at first, but it will improve rapidly if this process is continued a reasonable length of time and repeated at frequent intervals.

The rate of speed should be about twenty complete traced ovals and as many capitals to the minute.

LESSON 7

Review lesson 6.

To show the position at the desk as viewed from the rear, we here give another position illustration. Notice particularly the following points: There is some distance between the elbow and the side; the body is self-supporting in the chair; the eyes are fully fourteen inches from the paper; the hand is well up in front of the eyes, and the penholder points considerably to the right of the shoulder. In this position it is easy to acquire free muscular movement, and to learn to control it in a reasonably short time.

Students will notice that very much of the above is a repetition of preceding instructions. These details are of sufficient importance to merit constant repetition until they have been firmly fixed in the minds of students.

The propelling power is located behind the elbow. Do not forget this, and do not think of the energy and force as coming from the hand, fingers or wrist.

Following the plan suggested in connection with drill 5, the rotary motion should be applied in drill 6, below, the pen being in motion when striking the paper and in motion when leaving it. From 75 to 85 good capital A's should be made to the minute.

An Important Suggestion: Hold the practice paper in position with the left hand and always keep the paper in about the same relative position to the right arm. Move the paper from right to left and from left to right with the left hand, as may be required to keep the paper in good position.

Drill 6

LESSON 8

Begin with a careful examination of the conditions under which you are working. The position should be such that when you bend slightly at the hips the body will not come in contact with the desk. The right arm should be carried well out from the right side, and the right hand far enough in front of the eyes to form a right turn at the elbow. The side of the hand and the wrist must not touch the desk or paper, otherwise all motion from the muscles of the arm would stop at the wrist. The fingers must remain passive, no bending being permitted in the drills so far introduced. The pen must rest lightly and easily, but firmly, in the fingers. The propelling power is located back of the elbow.

MORE ROTARY MOTION

One of the best drills for beginners to practice in developing muscular movement is the large, compact oval which is given in number 7. Until these compact ovals have been mastered, and a rapid, light and elastic movement used in their execution, they may be profitably practiced a few minutes every day, but when the movement used in these drills has been mastered, it will be a waste of time to practice them more than two or three minutes at the beginning of every writing period. Every movement drill and every stroke of the pen in writing practice should have a direct bearing upon some letter or part of letter, and as soon as the end sought has been gained, the movement drill should be dropped for the more important work, that of developing the letter itself.

DRILL 7

A movement drill is a repeated form, and it may be a letter or a part of a letter, but it should be so simple in construction and susceptible of such ease in execution that the mind is relieved from the tedium of constantly dwelling upon the forms, and can be given to movement study.

In number 7 the movement used is in the direction of the capital O, and in order to make the oval very compact all strokes should be very light. One method used in making very compact ovals, is to first carry the ovals across the page with somewhat open spacing and go over the same path, again and again, until all white paper disappears. Through this process the fibre of the paper is not picked up by the points of the pen, and the final result is much more pleasing than it otherwise could be.

In number 7 not less than 185 downward strokes should be made in a minute.

The student should not forget that the compact oval exercise given above was made by a professional penman. This particular exercise was made with a finer pen then should be used in business writing. India ink, which produces a finer line than can be made with the ordinary fluids, was used, and more than an hour was consumed in its execution. It was, however, made with the same motion and at the same speed that students are instructed to use.

DRILL 8

The method of practice in drill 8 should be the same as in capital A, drill 5. After each traced oval lift the pen while in motion, swinging it below the base line and around to the beginning point of the capital O without checking the motion. Drive the pen rapidly, and bring the muscles of the arm into active play. First make ten revolutions for the traced oval, gradually decreasing the number to six; count six for the ovals and count two for each capital O.

DRILL 9

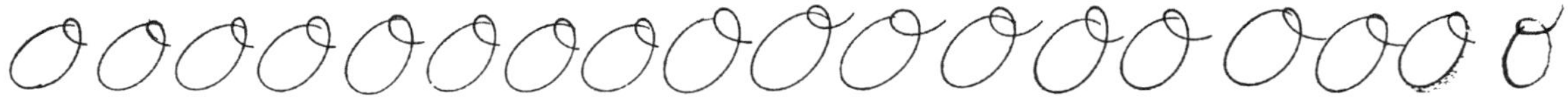

Not less than seventy of this form of capital O should be made in a minute.

This capital O is very popular with many excellent business penmen and teachers of modern writing. Study the letter and make a mental photograph of it. Note particularly the curves of the left and right sides; also the loop at the top, its general direction and its size.

LESSON 9

DRILL 10

This is a duplicate of drill 4 in lesson 6, and should be practiced in the same manner.

FOR STUDY

Drill 11

The plan of practice for drill 11 is the same as for drill 5, lesson 6, and drill 8, lesson 8.

Drill 12

Lift the pen from the paper while in motion in finishing a capital; continue the motion with the pen in the air and bring the pen to the paper to begin the next capital—all without checking the motion. Make about 70 letters to the minute.

LESSON 10

Drill 13

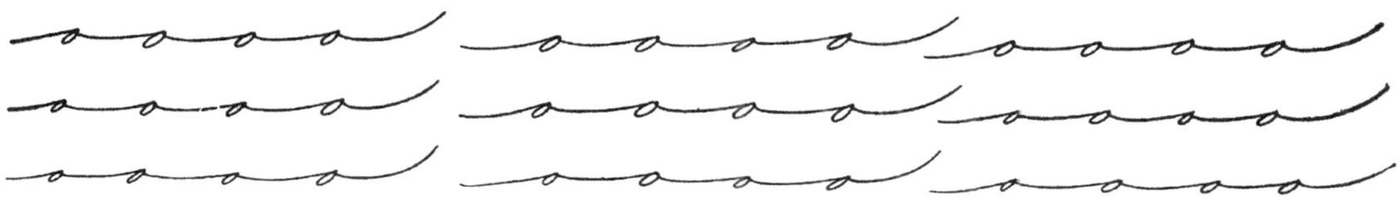

So far in the lessons the direct oval and some of its applications have been almost exclusively given as drills. In the connected small o just as much freedom of motion is necessary, but its operation should be in almost a straight line toward the right, thus developing the application of lateral movement used in such small letters as m, n, o, u, w.

The small o drill following should be practiced a few minutes every day during at least the first three months of a course in muscular movement writing. It can be made a very interesting drill.

In connection with this drill we urge teachers who have never tried the plan to use what we might term a conversational count. Walk about the room in time to the count of the letter, and in passing from desk to desk criticise the work being done by students in the same rythm. Supposing that passing down an aisle one student is making the o too large, another is not closing it at the top, another is using a slow, dragging movement, another is making a narrow, flat letter, and still another is bending over the desk too far, the criticisms would be as follows: Make "em" smaller, make "em" smaller; close "em" up, close "em" up; slide along, slide along; round "em" out, round "em" out; sit up, sit up. Each criticism or admonition may be repeated until the error has in a measure been corrected. The influence will not be lost upon the rest of the pupils, but those who have been making the same errors will, almost unconsciously, show a marked improvement.

DRILL 14

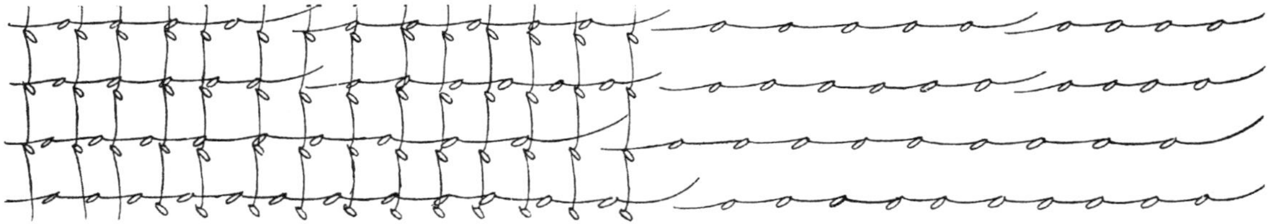

Make page after page of the connected small o, in the class and out of the class. Keep it up until you can make, with an easy, sliding movement, and nearly as well as the copy, more than 100 to the minute. That is by no means fast, but while permitting good form it is fast enough to force light movement.

To save paper, the small o may be made on the lines, between the lines and across the lines. The plan of writing across the lines is greatly to be commended and encouraged as tending to develop lightness and freedom of movement.

LESSON 11

DRILL 15

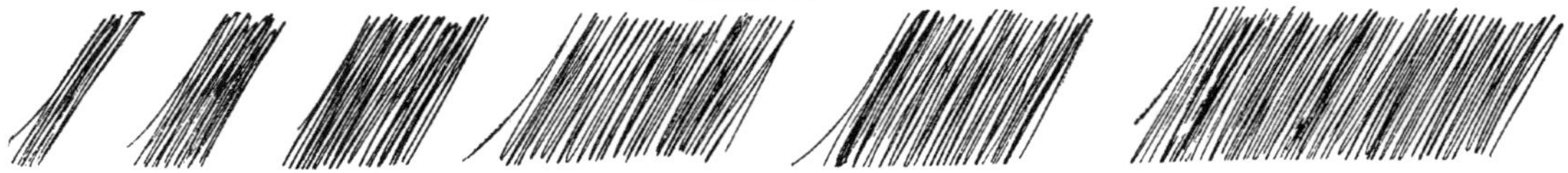

If all of the writing mechanism has been nicely adjusted, this exercise can be easily made. Before attempting to make the drill, see that the muscles of the right arm move easily. Remember that the larger part of the right arm just forward of the elbow, rests on the table; that the third and fourth fingers of the right hand are thrown (bent) well under; that the position of the pen in the hand is comfortable; that the right arm is well out from the side and the right hand well up in front of the eyes. Now push the hand forward and backward to test the freedom and movement power. If the muscles move easily, let the pen touch the paper, and move it lightly and rapidly over the paper. In this drill about 200 downward strokes should be made to the minute. Study, compare and practice.

MORE ABOUT COUNTING

In writing, as in music, regularity of movement is an important factor. A jerky, spasmodic motion is to be avoided, and successful teachers of writing have found that some method of marking the time of making the parts of letters is helpful. Some use a metronome, some a chalk box and a ruler, others use musical instruments; but we prefer that wonderful machine, the human voice, and a process of counting to fit the different parts or the letters. In individual home practice the counting process is of as much value as in the school room.

DRILL 16

In drill 15 no special effort is made to localize or control the movement, the one main object sought being to develop it. In No. 16 the results should be more open work, round turns at tops, angular connections at base, and light strokes throughout. A great many trials may be necessary before you can make anything resembling the copy. Count one for each downward stroke.

LESSON 12

Review lessons 5 and 6.

LESSON 13

Practice each of the following drills a few minutes, 5, 6, 13, 14 and 16.

LESSON 14

Open the lesson with a few minutes' practice of number 7 in lesson 8. Make the ovals somewhat open across the line once, and put them away to be continued at the opening of the next lesson.

DRILL 17

Preparatory to practice on number 17, test the movement by moving the pen in the air in the direction of the first stroke. Start the motion below the base line, and as the pen moves rapidly upward let it strike the paper at the beginning point. Drive the pen through the exercise rapidly and lightly. Do not make less than three connected m's before lifting the pen, and make more as soon as you have ability to make them well. You will make the letters too large, irregular and awkward at first, and you will have trouble with the union (connecting lines), but never mind, keep right on. All is well that ends well, and you will succeed if you persevere.

Not less than twenty completed exercises, or sixty small m's, should be made to the minute.

Bear in mind that an under stroke follows each m, the m proper being made with an over stroke.

Count 1, 2, 3, 1, 2, 3, 1, 2, 3, or 1, 2, 3, 4, 5, 6, 7, 8, 9.

LESSON 15

Make a line of compact ovals over those made in lesson 14, and again put the line away to be finished in the next writing period.

DRILL 18

In these small letter drills we have thought best to present a number of lines, thus showing by comparison the height of the letters, their width and general appearance in groups. For small m a count of three is used, and in the n a count of two; thus the count for drill 18 will be 1, 2, 1, 2, 1, 2, 1, 2, etc. Or for four connected letters, 1, 2, 3, 4, 5, 6, 7, 8. Relatively the speed should be the same as in the small m drill

LESSON 16

DRILL 19

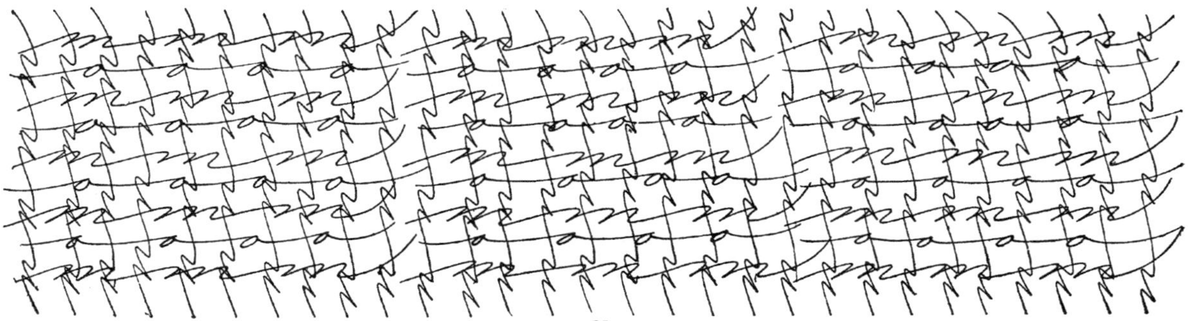

Return to the compact oval started in lesson 14 and continued in lesson 15. With a very light motion move the pen over the path of the preceding ovals again, and if the lines in all of the ovals are light and clear the result will be very attractive.

If the pen used is badly worn it should be changed.

Make the small m on a line across the page; then the small o across the page half way between the first and second lines. Continue half way down the page, turn the paper and make small n across the lines. This drill should be practiced often. This is drill 19, page 22.

LESSON 17

As opening exercises practice drills 4 and 5 in lesson 6.

DRILL 20

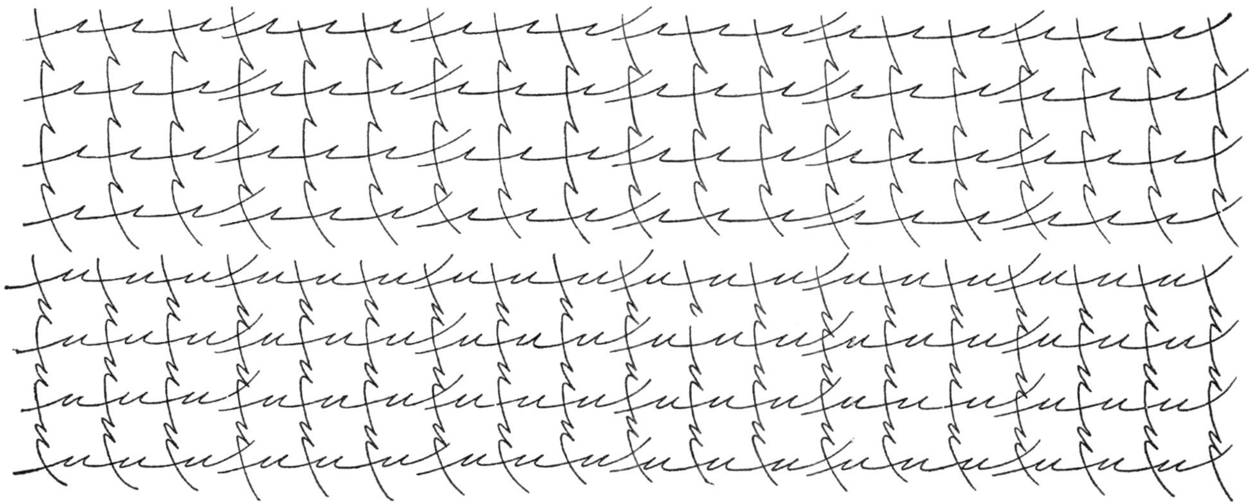

Small i and u are simple in construction. Study the letters and you will see how they are made. They should be sharp at top. Make a special study of the u, its width and connective lines.

LESSON 18

Again practice drills 5 and 6. Maintain a good position, use a light motion and make as many ovals and letters to a minute as can be made well.

DRILL 21

Here is our first word drill. *Take care of the movement and the letters will take care of themselves. Do not neglect the study of the motion and its application to the form to be made.*

Write the word Annum at the rate of sixteen or more words to a minute.

LESSON 19

As opening drills, practice drills 11 and 12 in lesson 9.

DRILL 22

Write the word Common at the rate of about eighteen to the minute.

LESSON 20

Open this lesson with drills 8 and 9 in lesson 8.

DRILL 23

Be sure that the motion is oval in its direction in starting the capital O. Move the pen in the air in the direction of the O. Let the pen, when moving rapidly downward, strike the paper.

If all conditions are favorable and the movement is free and firm, about twenty of the word Omen should be written in a minute.

LESSON 21

DRILL 24

Drill 24 may be used in developing small l and corresponding loops of small b, h, k and f, as well as small e. The object of the oval as a preparatory drill is twofold: First, to force the hand to move lightly and quickly, and second, to lead the motion in the direction of the letter itself. This is a good drill to practice often.

Capital M is a letter that affords splendid opportunity for the development of movement, and drill 25 leads up to it. For this drill count 1, 2, 3, 4, 5, 6, 7, and make twenty-five of the complete drills to the minute. Compare your work with the copy.

DRILL 25

Study the capital M closely before trying to make it. Compare the parts in their relation as regards height, slant and width. Make about forty letters to the minute, and count 1, 2, 3, 4 for each letter.

DRILL 26

LESSON 22

Review drills 24, 25 and 26 in lesson 21.

DRILL 27

In the capital M a count of four is used. There is one count less in the capital N. In practice work from fifty to sixty of these letters should be made to the minute. No especial effort should be made to form a loop at the junction of the first and last parts of capital N. Let that part of the letter take care of itself, but in size and general proportions the copy given should be closely imitated.

Remember that with a slow, dragging or cramped movement, nothing of lasting value can be accomplished in penmanship development.

LESSON 23

Review drills 25 and 26, lesson 21 and drill 27, lesson 22.

DRILL 28

In the practice of penmanship constant repetition is essential to success, and in connection with drill 28 the best results will be secured by practicing the word several minutes. At this stage of the work we prefer to have the students use the style of capital given in the copy, that in which the finishing stroke is carried below the base line and the pen lifted from the paper before the small letters are made. Later on the final stroke in capital M may connect directly with any small letters following.

LESSON 24

DRILL 29

Capitals M and N may be profitably practiced as movement drills at the beginning of this lesson. The word Noon will serve as a good movement drill if rightly practiced. Good practice speed, sixteen words to the minute.

LESSON 25

Drill 30 is one of the best drills so far given for the development of freedom and accuracy. Count as follows, C, 2, 3, 4, 5, 6, 7, 8, 9, 10, for each drill. The motion must be fast enough to produce smooth lines.

Drill 30

FOR STUDY

The small a is, in the main, a reduced copy of the capital A, and the first parts of small d and g are identical with small a. Fix the resemblance in the mind; it will help you. In business writing it is best to make the looped small d. It is just as legible and much faster than the stem. The loop to small g should be made without finger motion. We favor the blunt style in small g and y when they are final letters in a word. The small g thus made is identical with the figure 9.

Drill 31

It will pay to practice the small a drill a great deal. Try to make a half dozen or more lines of letters as small and as uniform as the copy. Students should not forget to study the copy constantly and to make frequent comparisons of their work with the copy. A count of two should be used for each small a, and in connecting five letters it is a good plan to count ten. From seventy to eighty small a's should be made to the minute, where five are connected as shown above.

LESSON 26

As an opening drill, practice drill 19, lesson 16.

DRILL 32

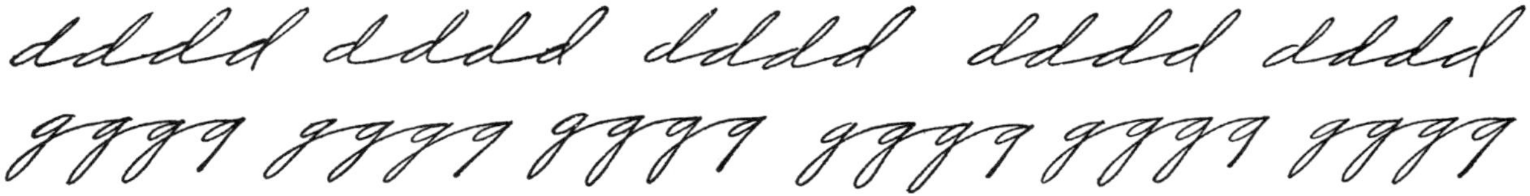

Practice on such words as good, dug, dog, and gad after small d and g have received careful attention.

Do not lose sight of the fact that all of these exercises are given not only to train the muscles, but to train the eye. If you have patiently and persistently followed the course so far and are not able to make the exercises and words with uniformity, do not be discouraged. The first step is to acquire a light, elastic movement, and while the letters at first may appear very irregular and the movement may be erratic, there is no cause for discouragement.

In the style of writing here presented the loop of small g extends three spaces below the base line. The paper should be held in such a position that the downward strokes are pulled toward a point central between the eyes, the paper being changed from time to time with the left hand to keep its position relatively the same. The motion should be purely muscular throughout, and the movement in making the loop particularly quick and elastic. Study the form closely and note the crossing of the loop with a left curve on the base.

In groups of four connected letters a speed of sixty-four letters to the minute should be attained. A count of two for each letter and a count of eight for each group of four will aid in regulating the movement.

LESSON 27

As an opening drill practice drill 10 in lesson 9.

DRILL 33

The basis of all extended loop letters is the small l, and it cannot be questioned that time expended in its mastery will be time well spent.

HEIGHT—Where such a style of penmanship as is represented by these copies is adopted, the loops may extend a trifle more than three spaces high, some choosing to make them even four spaces. (By a space is meant the height of your minimum letters). It is of little importance whether you make them three, three and one-half, or four spaces in height, so long as the chief rule is observed, viz.: *To keep them uniform in length*. However, where the ruling of the paper is narrow, loops should be made short enough to avoid running into the line above or below.

MOVEMENT USED—In business writing all loops below the line should be made with pure muscular movement. In making those above the line the fingers should be relaxed, and as the arm slides forward a slight extension of the fingers will prove beneficial in executing the upper part of the loop. The combination of the two movements is perfectly natural to most hands, and little encouragement need be given to the use of the fingers. The student must guard against falling entirely back upon the finger movement. Keep an eye on your wrist to see that it moves forward and backward in unison with the other movements. Under no circumstances allow the fleshy part of the hand forward of the wrist to rest.

Practice upon drill 33 until you can produce it rapidly, easily and with a good degree of accuracy. If this is your first special work on loops do not expect to master them in a day. A month will be soon enough.

CAUTIONS—You will find your first difficulty in getting enough curve on the upward stroke. A half hour's determined practice will do much to overcome this tendency. Keep the paper at such an angle before the body as will make the loops, generally speaking, run straight toward the middle of the body. ABOVE ALL, KEEP THEM THE SAME HEIGHT, ON UNIFORM SLANT AND EQUAL DISTANCE APART, AND DON'T SHADE.

DRILL 34

Slide forward on the third and fourth fingers as the loop is formed and draw the hand straight on main slant to base line. Do not keep the fingers rigid. Count one for every l made. Make at least eighty small l's to the minute where two are joined, and, applying the same speed, more, of course, may be made when the pen is not lifted so often.

Study the results of your work from all positions. Turn your letters sidewise and bottom side up and compare with the copy. If they tip over too much, it is an indication that not enough curve has been used in the first stroke, and that you must curve it more.

Devote as much time as possible outside of school hours to practice on the loops.

LESSON 28

DRILL 35

In the preceding lesson some attention was given to the development of the loop letters, but not enough. Study the relation of the loop to the oval, as shown in the first line of drill 35.

The letters given here are of about the right length for average business writing. There is a slight checking of the motion on the downward strokes, but not enough to stop the motion at the base line. After a little practice, loops as good as the above in groups of five should be made at the rate of from 125 to 150 to the minute. The author's average practice speed is 140.

LESSON 29

DRILL 36

More study, more practice. Study and practice should be inseparable companions in developing good writing. One without the other will lead to one-sided results. Don't be one-sided.

A nice movement drill is embodied in the above. Close observation will indicate just how it is done. The small traced oval is about one-half the capital in height, and the upper loop is one-half the entire height of the letter. If you have a sharp eye and a responsive mind you have been able to grasp these details without any suggestions from the author, and you have gone farther. You have noted the curve in the main downward stroke, the flatness of the lower loop on the base line, and the dropping of the finishing stroke below the base.

DRILL 37

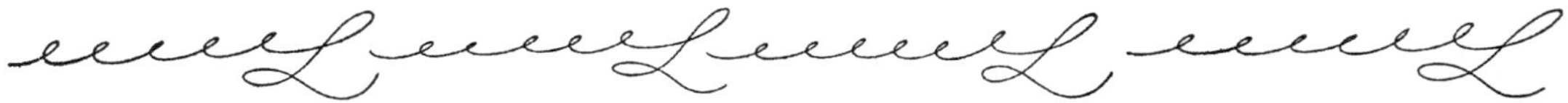

Look at it. A little e one-half the distance from the base line to the top of the capital L. Don't falter, but use a light, quick, gliding movement.

DRILL 38

See how lightly you can carry the pen over the paper. Barely let the points of the pen touch it. Make a test of the movement with the pen above the paper, and when fully ready for action make from sixty to seventy good letters to the minute.

LESSON 30

Review lesson 29 before practicing the following words:

DRILL 39

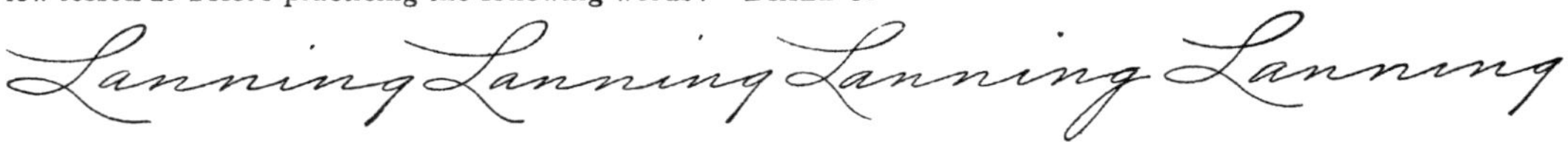

DRILL 40

Practice drills 39 and 40 at fifteen or more words to the minute.

Leisure Moment Drills.—To be used for class work at option of the teacher

DRILL 41

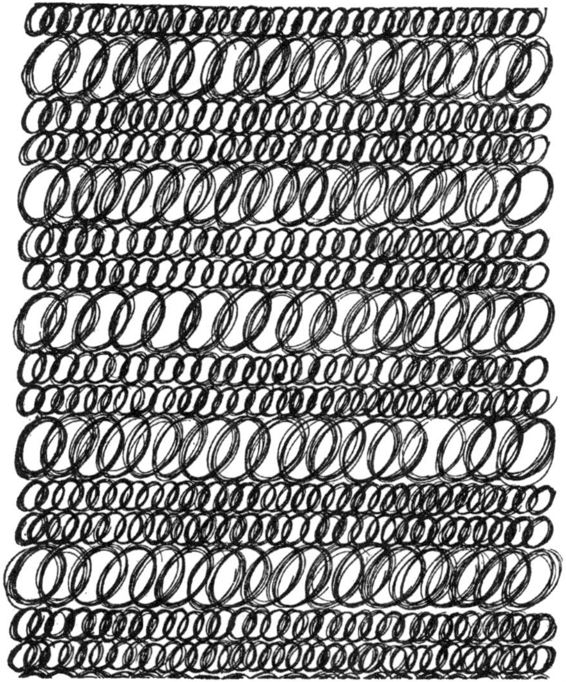

On this page are given engraved specimens of students' practice sheets on ovals. These are only one-half the originals in size, as it was necessary to reduce the students' pages one-half to bring them within the limits of a page. It is not expected that students practicing from these lessons will make more than a few lines of each copy at the beginning of any lesson. Keep the pages thus begun and fill in the lines as you have the time. Make your ovals twice the size of those given here.

DRILL 42

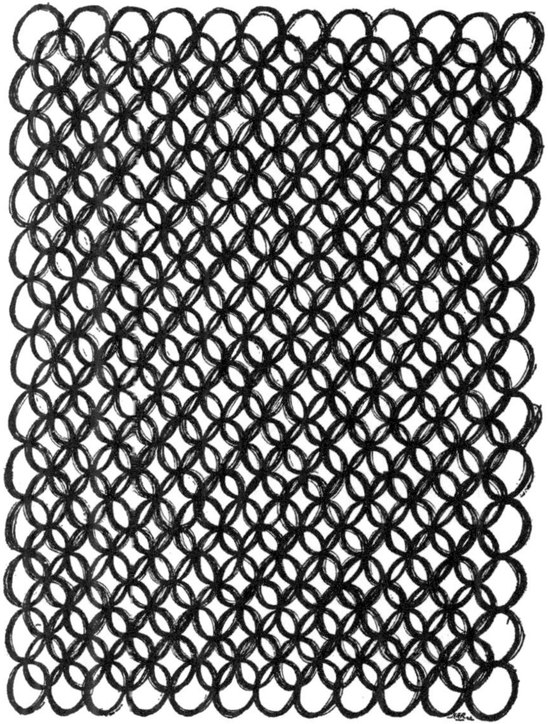

LESSON 31

Drill 43

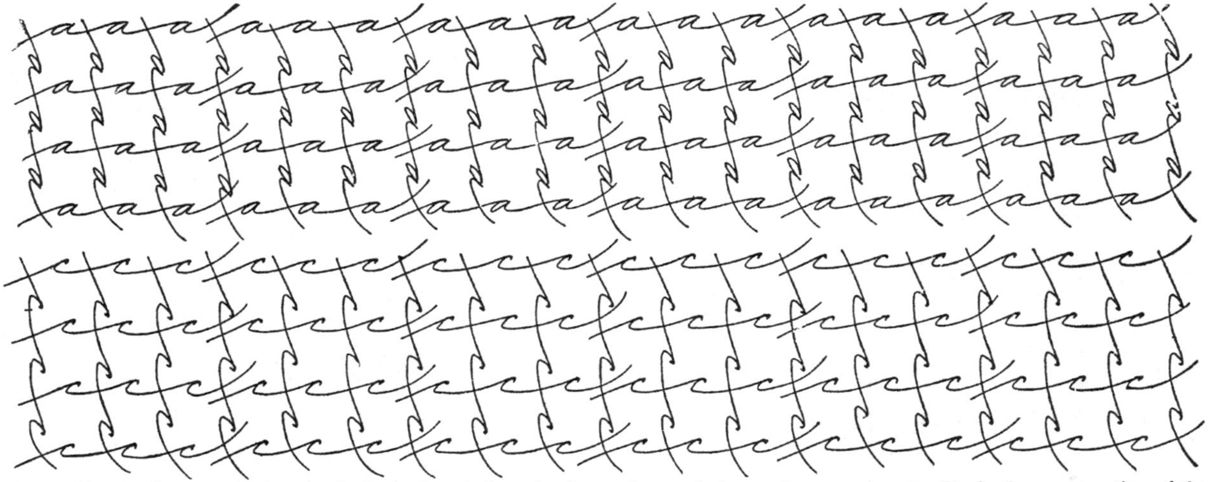

In small c the first part of the small a is the foundation, the dot at the top being an important part. Study the construction of the letter carefully before practicing it.

LESSON 32

Drill 44

The style of small r given in the preceding page is not a letter that can be made at a high rate of speed. The form requires a checking of the movement at the top to admit of forming a shoulder. Study the parts of the letter shown before the first completed form. Seventy good letters to the minute is a fair rate of speed, and a complete mastery of the form will require frequent drills.

The following form can be made at a much higher rate of speed, and while somewhat difficult to learn, is much easier in execution when mastered.

The first stroke in this letter in drill 45 is very much like the first part of small m or n. The downward stroke is retraced to a point about one-fourth of a space above the first part; a stop (hardly noticeable) and a dot are made before the swinging curve to the next letter. Close study of the form while practicing will be necessary. After its mastery, one hundred connected letters to the minute will be a good rate of speed. The first few trials will unquestionably be discouraging, but faithful practice will be rewarded. Stick to it.

DRILL 45

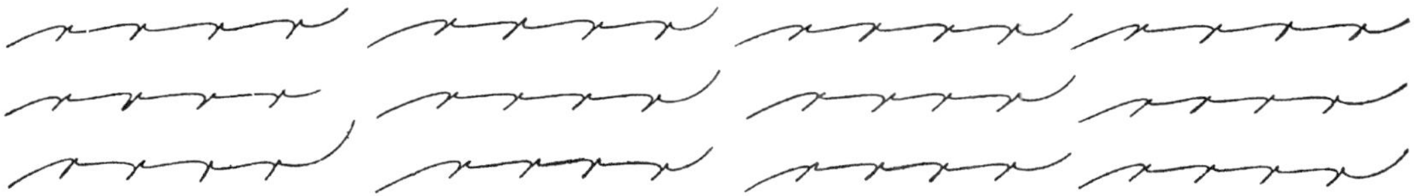

DRILL 46

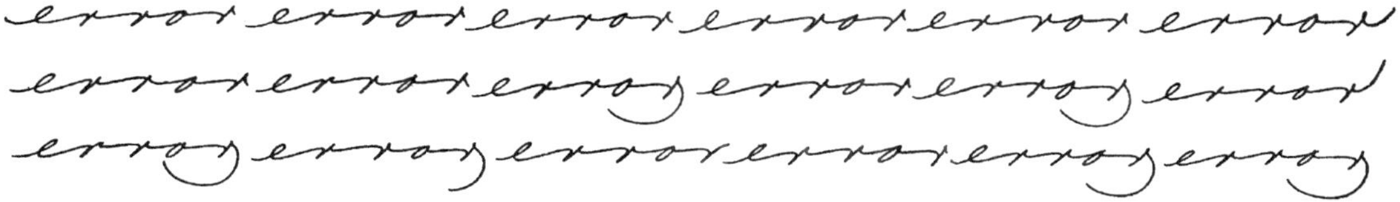

Practice speed in this drill from twenty to twenty-four words to the minute.

LESSON 33

Open the lesson with oval and small o movement drills.

Small s is a companion to the small r given in drill 44. Both letters are usually made a little higher than other small letters of the same class, such as o, m, n, etc., not because there is any technical rule for making them higher, but because it is generally agreed that they look better in words when so made.

Small s should be pointed at the top and closed on the base line. An easy, sliding and light motion should be used.

Review drill 45 as a part of this lesson if time permits.

Drill 47

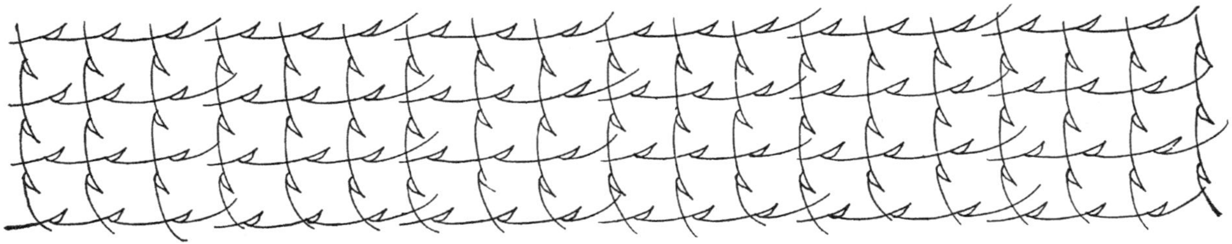

LESSON 34

Drill 48

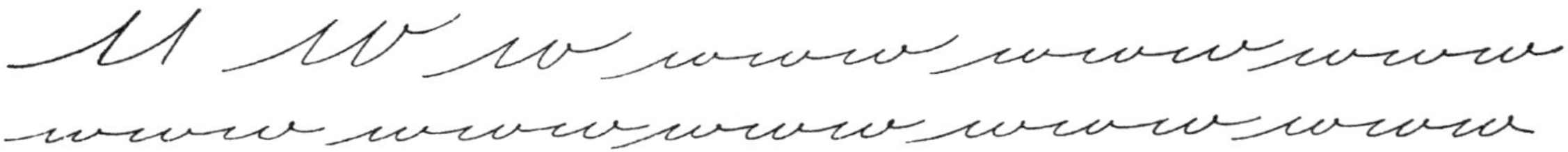

Small u is the basis of the small w. Study the enlarged forms.

Calling the distance between the upper points of small u one space, the finishing stroke in w should be carried one-half space to the right of second point. Compare your work with the copy at frequent intervals. Count 1, 2, 3, 1, 2, 3, etc.

Drill 49

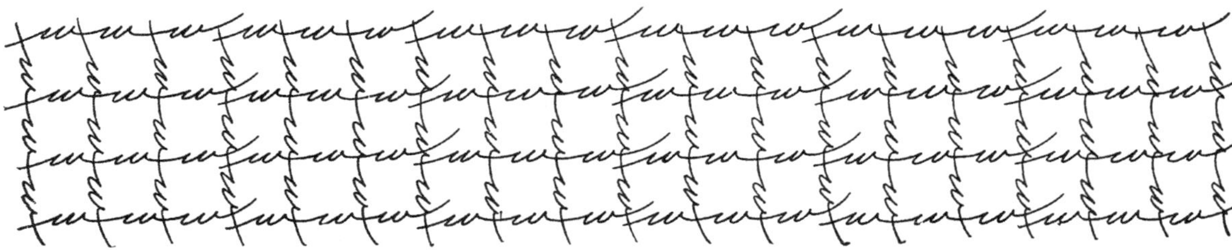

LESSON 35

For movement practice, review drills 11 and 12 in lesson 9.

DRILL 50

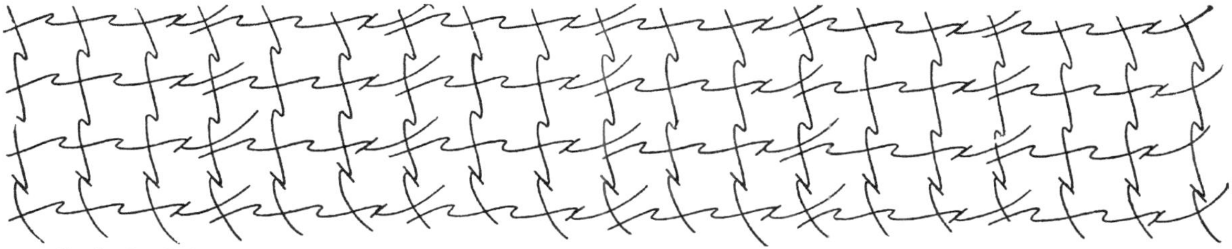

The small x is simple in construction. Study it. The cross stroke may be made either upward or downward, but the author prefers the upward stroke. Use the main slant in this line, that is the same slant as is used in all main downward strokes in the small letters.

LESSON 36

Practice drill 30 in lesson 25, and drill 45 in lesson 32.

DRILL 51

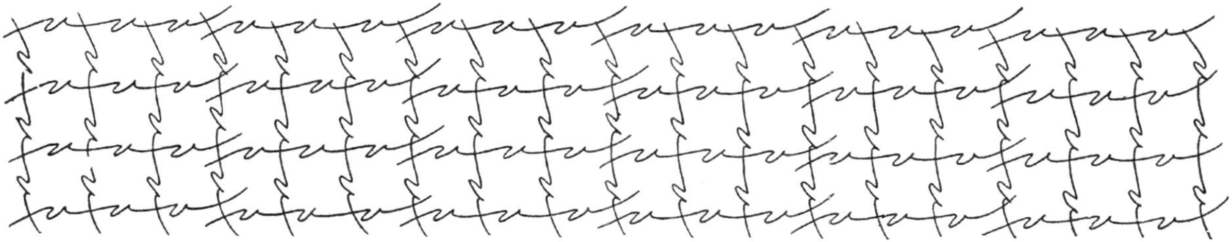

The first part of small v is the same in form as the first part of small x given in drill 50. Small v must be open at the top. Students should compare their letters with the copy often.

LESSON 37

Practice number 19 as an opening drill. Study the enlarged form of the small h. The first part is the small l brought straight to base. Study the joining of the first and last parts. A count of eight can be used to advantage for each group of four letters.

While there should be a continual sliding of the hand in this drill, producing nearly pure muscular movement, a very slight bending of the fingers as the turns are made at top is permissible in all loops.

DRILL 52

The small y is the small h upside down. Reverse the page, and let drill 52 serve as a copy for practice on small y.

DRILL 53

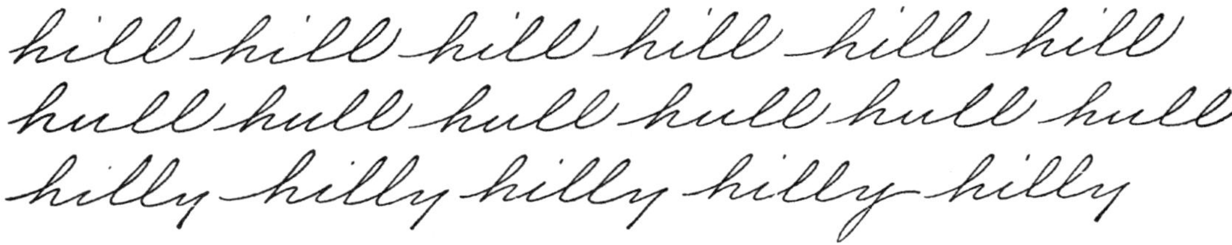

The rate of practice speed should be about twenty-five of the words hill or hull, and twenty or more of the word hilly in a minute.

LESSON 38

REVERSE OVAL AND DIRECT APPLICATION

An application of the reverse oval motion is made in forming the capital J. Study number 54. The reverse oval, it must be understood, begins with an upward stroke on the left side. Before attempting the capital J make reverse ovals four or five minutes, and if the movement is then light and uniform, this copy may be safely practiced. The oval, in connection with capital J, is used as a driving force.

DRILL 54

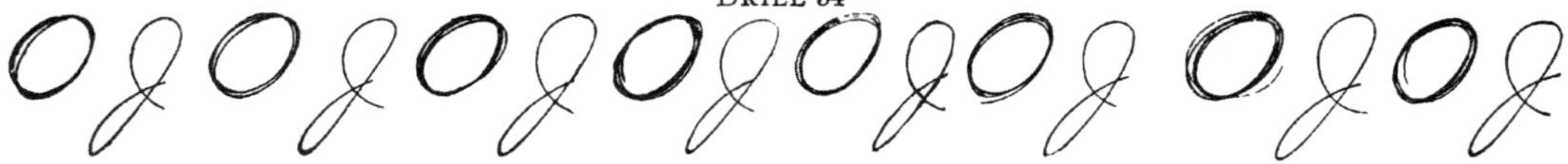

Make the oval in a count of six, lift the pen from the paper at the top, and without checking the motion, swing the pen in its natural course in the air to the right and below the base to the point of contact with the paper in starting the letter. Do not stop the motion, but strike the paper in an upward course at full speed for the beginning stroke of J. If the explanation of applied motion is not fully understood, study it until it is, and then fill at least a half page with the copy.

Do not neglect the form, but note carefully the following points: The J should begin with an upward stroke from a point just below the base line; the turn at the top should be round; the upper part should be about one space longer and twice the width of the lower part.

DRILL 55

Slant may be troublesome. If so, study and practice this copy faithfully. It will help you.

DRILL 56

This copy is given as a drill on both movement and form. From the beginning stroke of J to the finishing stroke of s the pen should not be lifted. Write the word from beginning to end with a steady, light and uniform movement. Eighteen or twenty words to the minute will be a fair rate of practice speed.

LESSON 39

DRILL 57

The count for this drill is 1, 2, 3, 4, 5, 6, 7, 8; two for the capital I and six for the oval drill. Capital I begins in same manner as capital J, but the upper part is narrower. Write fifteen or twenty lines of this copy before passing to the next.

Drill 58

Not less than fifty of this capital to the minute. The count is two for each letter.

Drill 59

The angular finish in this letter is of especial value when small letters follow, as shown in the following lesson.

LESSON 40

Review lesson 39.

Drill 60

This is a medium hand, but it is often necessary to write more compactly. Other words in which the small letters already practiced are used, may be introduced for practice.

THE FREQUENCY OF REVIEWS

The author is unable to decide at what points in the course reviews should be given. The matter of review must be dependent upon the thoroughness with which the lessons have been mastered in their regular order.

The ability of students to use and apply muscular movement as explained in the preceding lessons should determine the review question. In classes of average ability a week spent in review at this stage of the work would, without question, be profitable.

Starting from the movement drills given in these lessons, it is often a good plan to encourage students to give full play to their inventive and constructive ability in adapting the drills to different designs. Such work, however, should be largely done outside of school hours. Hanging on the walls of one of the author's school rooms are a great variety of such designs sent him from a school where his lessons have been used. In the drills mentioned are mainly used the straight line, compact, open and interlaced oval, large and small, the small m, n, e, o, c, l, h and b. Among these designs are houses, carriages, crosses, battleships and many curious designs which we do not find names for. Many are worked out in colored inks and the effects on the whole are pleasing.

Herewith we give a drill that is a favorite exercise with many teachers. In this drill students should be permitted to use pencil outlines to indicate the length of the lines and width of ovals.

LESSON 41 DRILL 61

In this and the following lesson are given reviews of what are termed the minimum or one-space letters. As has been stated, these letters are all of the same height except r and s, and in the style of writing taught in these lessons a space in height approximates one-sixteenth of an inch. The small r given in drill 45, lesson 32, should be substituted for the style given above.

LESSON 42 DRILL 62

LESSON 43

DRILL 63

This copy will furnish all the movement drill necessary in beginning this lesson. Count ten for each drill, two for the capital S and eight for the reverse traced oval. About sixteen completed drills should be made to the minute. This drill is especially recommended to those who find the development of a light, quick movement difficult.

DRILL 64

Study the first form closely; it is for the purpose of study. Study the curve of the first stroke; study the loop at the top and give especial attention to the fact that the loop (upper part of S) is one-half the entire length of the letter. With an easy, light movement make from fifty to sixty letters to the minute.

DRILL 65

The angular finishing stroke shown in drill 65 is very popular with many excellent teachers of business writing. Nearly as high a rate of speed can be attained in its execution as in the preceding form, drill 64. Its practical feature is the direction taken by the finishing stroke, which may be joined to any letter following.

LESSON 44

Review lesson 43.

DRILL 66

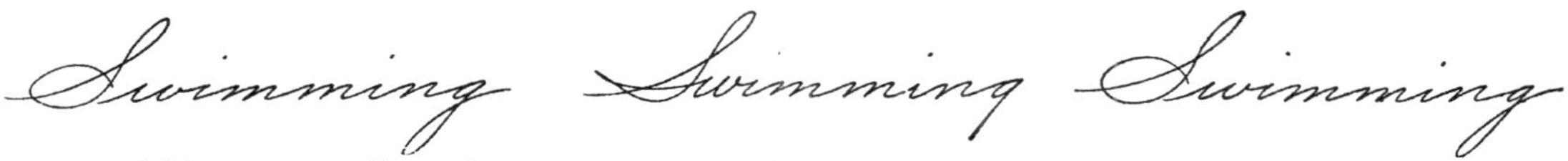

Write a page of this copy; more if you have at your command sufficient time. A continuous steady movement should be used. Do not lift the pen from the beginning of the small w to the ending line in g.

LESSON 45

DRILL 67

In this drill the capital G is made first in a count of three, followed by the reverse traced oval, from six to ten revolutions.

DRILL 68

Study the form closely before attempting to make it; be sure that you not only know when you make a poor letter, but you know why it is poor. One bad stroke may spoil an otherwise good letter. Learn to locate the bad strokes. Make from forty to fifty letters to the minute

DRILL 69

This is a good business form. Extended instruction is unnecessary. Use your eyes.

DRILL 70

The angular finishing stroke gives a connective line for any letter that may follow, and admits of joining the capitals for an extended drill as well.

LESSON 46

Review lesson 45.

DRILL 71

Nothing can be better at this stage of the work than easy words constantly repeated. Through a series of repetitions, strength in movement is developed, and faults become prominent.

LESSON 47

CAUTION TO THE STUDENT

Never begin to practice until you are sure you know how to practice. Languid, thoughtless practice should be avoided. Put ambition, put energy, put the fire of determined will behind your practice, and the results will be astonishing. Take advantage of all favorable conditions. Keep not only the muscles of the right arm in a relaxed condition, but guard against tense muscles in any part of the body. Keep the side of the hand and the wrist free from the desk; keep the right arm well out from the side; keep the right hand in front of the eyes; keep a right angle at the right elbow, and remember that the propelling power is located back of the right elbow. If you think you are in a good position for writing, test the movement without touching the pen to the paper, and while doing this, study the conditions under which you are trying to work. Be sure you are right before you go ahead.

DRILL 72

Not much movement drill of a special character is necessary in opening this lesson, the connected small p affording an excellent exercise. Study the form with care. Note particularly the point at the top and the loop below the base line, the length above and below base, and the point of intersection (crossing) of the lower part and the main downward stroke.

In the above is given a particularly excellent drill, to be made with pure muscular movement.

From sixty to sixty-six connected letters should be made to the minute. Make frequent comparisons and write a page.

DRILL 73

Average rate of speed for the above, twenty words to the minute.

DRILL 74

Write about fourteen words to the minute of copy 74

LESSON 48

DRILL 75

Make a few letters in the air as a preliminary movement drill before beginning active work. As will be readily seen, nearly all the main oval part is at the left of the beginning stroke. The count is two, and from fifty to sixty letters should be made to the minute. Make a full page and practice steadily, not spasmodically.

DRILL 76

Make also a page of this letter. It is a good movement drill. Count three, and be sure to connect the last part with the first, in a loop a little above the center of the letter. From forty-five to fifty good letters should be made to the minute.

DRILL 77

A good movement drill; study it and practice it with a light, quick movement.

LESSON 49

Review lesson 48.

DRILL 78

Write from twelve to fifteen words to the minute, and five words should be written on a line of average foolscap length. This is a good movement drill if properly practiced.

LESSON 50

BUSINESS FIGURES

Nothing within the range of business writing is more important to the average bookkeeper or office clerk than good figures. In many lines of accounting thousands of business figures are made without the writing of a single word.

This, in a measure, is true in many branches of statistical work connected with railroad bookkeeping where headings are printed and page after page is filled with figures. The first requisite is legibility, and its importance cannot be emphasized too much. While in writing the letters in a word, each may be known by the context, in making figures, each must depend upon itself for legibility. How important then that each figure should be so formed that its value, in a group or by itself, cannot be mistaken. In this connection attention is directed to the word Communication and the figures preceding and following that word. Any one who is able to read fairly will not hesitate to pronounce this word communication at a glance, and yet there are very few letters in the word that are really used in spelling it; the m's being pointed at the top and thus easily mistaken for i's or e's, while the "n" is a small u pure and simple.

FOR STUDY

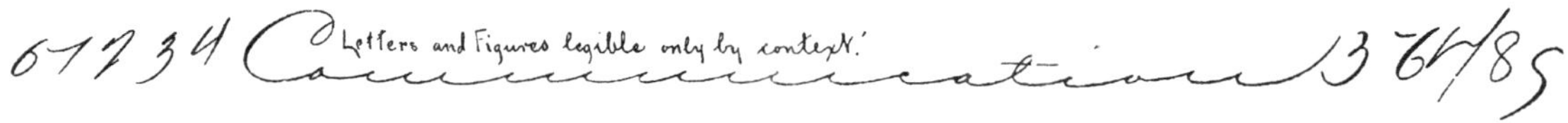

A great many who are considered good business writers become careless in their writing and adopt the under motion, which sharpens the m's and n's at the top; this same carelessness in constructing figures will lead to the most serious results. Examine the groups of figures preceding and following the word communication. The cipher looks more like a 6 than naught, while the 1 is clearly a figure 7; then the figure which is intended for the 2 could easily be mistaken for the figure 7, while the 3 and 4 are fairly plain. The 5 in a column would be added as a 3 and the 7 might be mistaken for the figure 4. Let us emphasize, then, the desirability of making only the plainest kind of figures, those that cannot be mistaken for figures which they are not intended to represent.

FOR STUDY

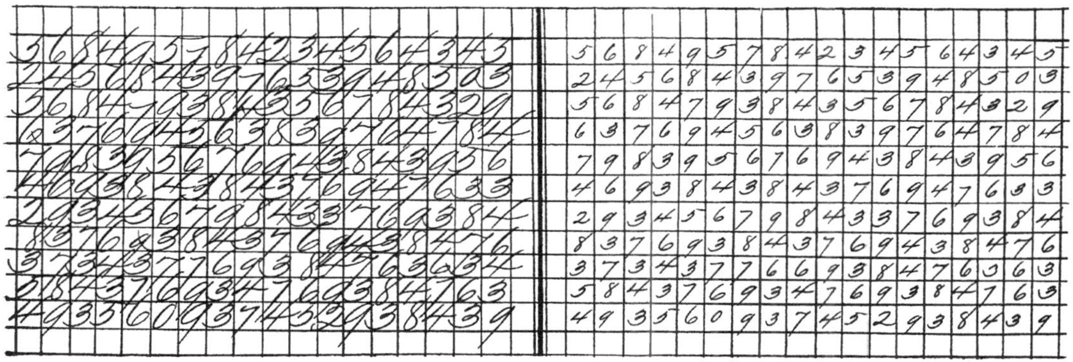

Figures should be made small, students sometimes think that large figures are necessarily the plainest, but such is not the case. Examine carefully the diagram presented herewith. At the left are figures that are absolutely plain; one could not be mistaken for another, and yet their extreme size in the space in which they are placed make them difficult to read. At the right are the same figures made no better, but a great deal smaller. Please note carefully the fact that these, surrounded as they are by white paper, and much smaller, are much more legible, even at a distance, than are the large figures at the left.

Students who have practiced in copybooks have almost invariably acquired the habit of making figures three or four times too large. Those that we present for models from which to practice are large enough for ordinary use. If occasion demands it will be easy to make the figures larger. One-eighth of an inch is perhaps high enough for ordinary figures, while in some places it would be advantageous to make them even smaller.

FOR STUDY

FORM

Naught, a disconnected small o, always closed at the top; one, a plain oblique straight line; two, a small loop or a dot in beginning, a full right curve to base, and a small loop flat on base; three, beginning with dot, upper part about one-third entire size, made with a great deal of side motion; four, oblique straight line, horizontal straight line finished with a slight left curve extending a little above the first part and resting on the base line; five, beginning with plain downward oblique line, well rounded in main part, and with the horizontal line at top always connected with first part; six may extend above the other figures, and should always be finished with a small loop, the finishing point being brought to base line each time. There are no angles in the form of seven given here. A more graceful form could have been produced had two angular turns been made, one at extreme upper left and other at extreme upper right point, but such a form sacrifices speed while gaining nothing in legibility. Figure seven extends below the base line. Our figure eight begins at the upper left side, while some who make this figure well begin on opposite side. The upper part of figure nine rests on base line, with stem extending below. Close the upper part.

HOW TO PRACTICE

In making the figure one, draw the hand toward you with a quick, light motion, sliding on the third and fourth fingers. Uniformity in height and slant are the two important points to observe.

The development and application of a lateral oval motion will aid in the construction of the figure two. In making the figure two in class drill a count of three should be used, one, two, three, one, two, three, etc., or dot, two, three.

Notice the exercise preceding the figure three. The motion used in that exercise will produce a good figure three if properly applied; one, two, three, or dot, two, three, is the count used. A count of three is also used in four and five, but for six, seven and nine, a count of two.

Several lessons should be given to drilling on the figures singly before grouping them, but as soon as the forms are mastered and the student can make them at a fair rate of speed, it is best to drill in a miscellaneous order somewhat as follows: 1, 0, 2, 6, 9. 8, 5, 4, 3, 0, 9, 6, 7, 2, 8, 9, 3, 5, 6, 9, 2, 1, 5, 8, 6, 9, 5, 4, 6, 9, 3, 7, 8, etc. No particular order is necessary, but the aim should be to repeat one figure as often as another.

RATE OF SPEED

Figures taken singly, 175 ones, 150 naughts, 80 twos, 75 threes, 80 fours, 75 fives, 100 sixes, 95 sevens, 90 eights and 100 nines per minute. Figures taken promiscuously, not less than 95 good figures to the minute. This rate can be increased materially by repeated effort. Persistence brings success. Practice steadily and faithfully.

DRILL 79

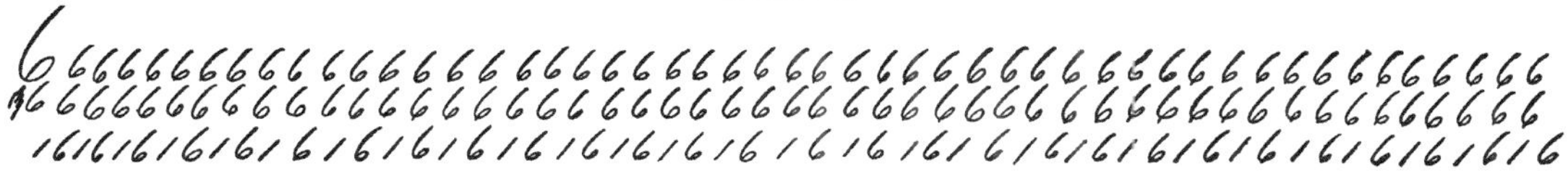

LESSON 51 DRILL 80

It is truly interesting to watch the development and improvement in figure practice in a class where the work is well and systematically done. At this stage of the work a full week should be devoted to this practice, and there should be frequent reviews.

Some teachers place great emphasis upon the order of simplicity, but, as a matter of fact, there can be no well defined order of simplicity, as hardly two students will be able to agree on figures that are easy and those that are hard to master, and since we are going to devote some time to drill on each figure during a period of one week there is little use of attempting any arrangement on the basis of simplicity. If there is a difference, the difficult figures should be practiced the most.

DRILL 81

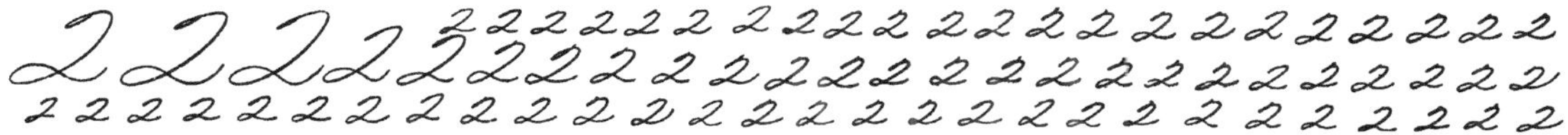

As soon as fair progress has been made in the constructive part of the 2, an effort should be made to bring the rate of speed up to eighty to the minute. Count one, two, three, or dot, two, three, for each figure made in class practice.

LESSON 52 DRILL 82

The method here presented has proven more satisfactory in the author's classes than any other that he has tested in teaching **figure 8.** The motion produces the figure; learn the motion thoroughly. Count one, two, three, or dot, two, three, and make from seventy to eighty figures to the minute.

DRILL 83

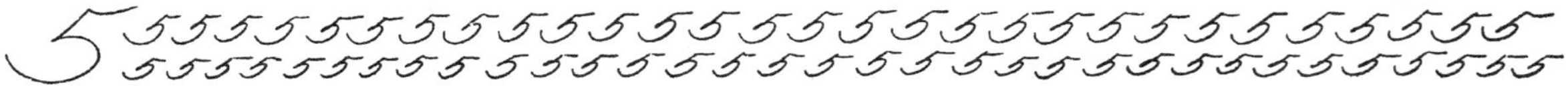

Figure 5 is in a large measure dependent upon the horizontal stroke at the top for its legibility. Study the form as well as practice it. About seventy good figures should be made to the minute. This speed may be increased later on. Count one, two, three.

LESSON 53

DRILL 84

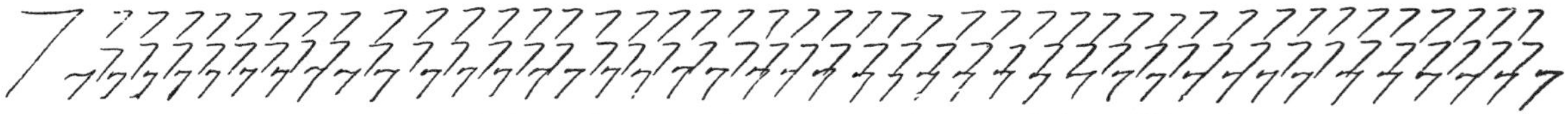

Seven extends below the base. Make this figure in count of one, two, at the rate of about 100 to the minute.

LESSON 54

DRILL 85

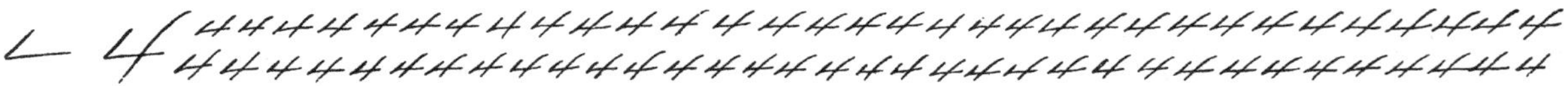

The four rests on the base line, and usually the last part extends above the first part. Count one, two, three, and make from seventy to eighty to the minute.

LESSON 55

DRILL 86

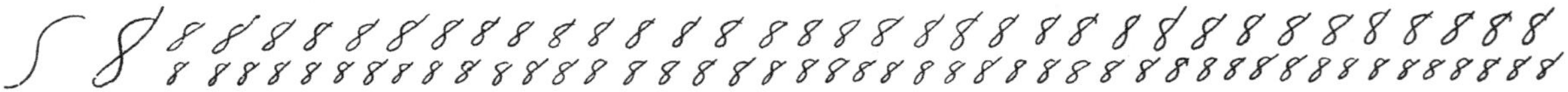

After a few minutes drill on figure 8, miscellaneous figures should be introduced. In class work these figures should be made from the dictation of the teacher, and the practice speed should be from 90 to 100 figures to the minute. The author usually makes the figures on the blackboard as they are dictated to the class. A fairly rapid penman can make from 100 to 125 good figures on the blackboard to the minute. Make ninety eights to the minute.

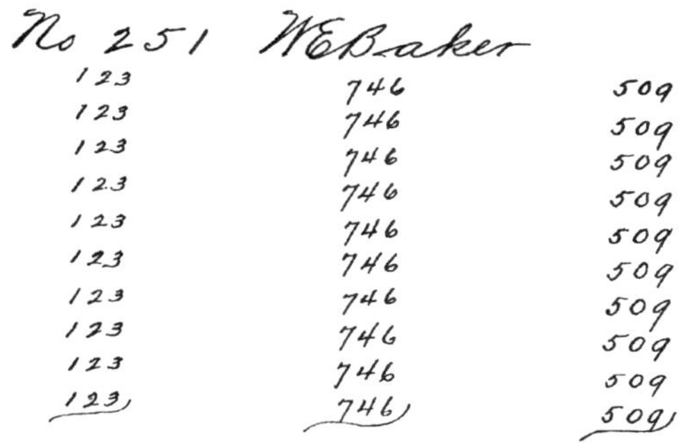

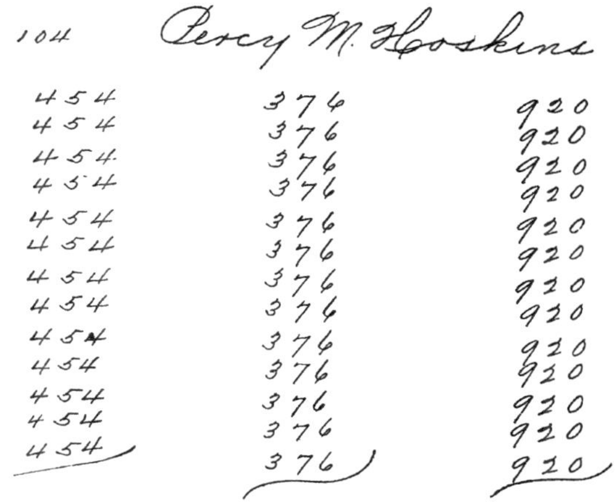

STUDENTS' WORK IN FIGURES

On this page are printed as models, figures executed rapidly by students. These figures are especially commended because of their extreme legibility, their neatness and the evident rapidity with which they were made. What one student has accomplished another can.

LESSON 56

DRILL 87

As a movement drill, practice the traced ovals as given in the second study in drill 87. Also practice the last four letters with the traced ovals. The remaining part of the drill is for study only.

SPECIAL POINTS TO OBSERVE

Capital E is made with an application of the oval motion, as developed in the capitals O, A and C, the application varying but little.

The upper part of capital E is about one-third the entire height of the letter. The finishing oval should not exceed one-half the entire height and the loop marking two-thirds the height of the letter points downward at about a right angle with the main slant as shown by the straight lines in the fourth form.

Drill 88

Careful study and practice of this copy will aid the development of the form. Compare the upper and lower traced ovals especially as related to size. Count six for each traced oval and move the pen lightly and rapidly.

Drill 89

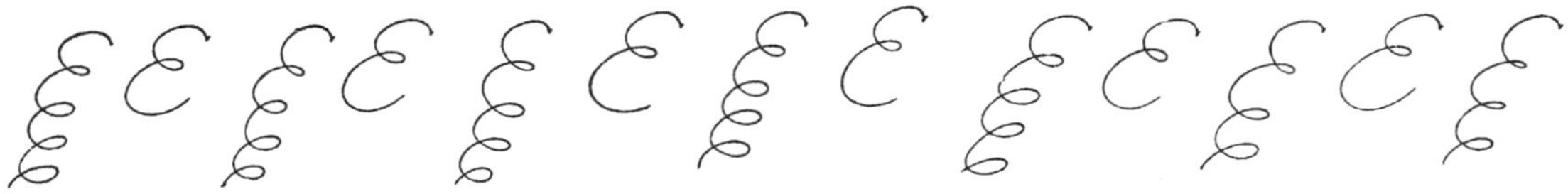

Still more study, and still more practice. Let study and practice move together along parallel lines. The capital E here given begins with a dot. For rapid business writing we consider it the best.

Drill 90

This copy is both for study and practice.

Drill 91

A count of three should be used for the capital E. In counting for this form of letters in class drills the author counts dot, two, three, dot, two, three, etc.

Drill 92

The value of this drill in the plan of development cannot be questioned. It should be practiced earnestly.

LESSON 57

DRILL 93

The framework of capital B is clearly shown in the models above given. The straight line starting at a point about three-fourths of the distance from the base to the top of the letter is purely a guide line; a prop upon which the remainder of the letter rests. Without it, beginners make very feeble letters and slow progress. Although usually lost in the retraced lines of the first part, the author considers it a very essential part of the letter. If the above forms are closely studied and practiced, the following copies will be comparatively easy.

DRILL 94

Definiteness is essential in business writing. There should be a definite starting point and a definite ending point in every letter. Every curve and every loop should be definite and have a definite place in the process of construction. In studying the forms of the letters here given, bear this in mind. Capital B may end in a dot as shown in the greater number of the letters given above, and it may end in an angular turn, furnishing a connective stroke for the letters following, as shown in the third and fourth letters in drill 93.

The count for capital B is 1, 2, 3, and a fair practice speed is fifty to the minute when the letters are disconnected as above, and a little higher rate of speed when the letters are connected as in drill 95

DRILL 95

LESSON 58

Review lessons 27 and 28.

LESSON 59

Practice, two or three minutes only, drills 4 and 5, lesson 6, and drill 6, lesson 7.

Study the enlarged form of small b. The lower part of the letter should be as wide as the loop through its widest part, and some good writers make it a little wider. Do not make your letters larger than those in the copy. Make line after line of the small b until you are able to make it easily and at a fair rate of speed. Twenty groups of 100 letters to the minute is not a high rate of speed for this drill. Perhaps ninety to the minute will be fast enough for the average pupil.

DRILL 96

The count for each group should be 1, 2, 3, 4, 5, 6, 7, 8, 9, 10.

LESSON 60

Review lesson 59.

DRILL 97

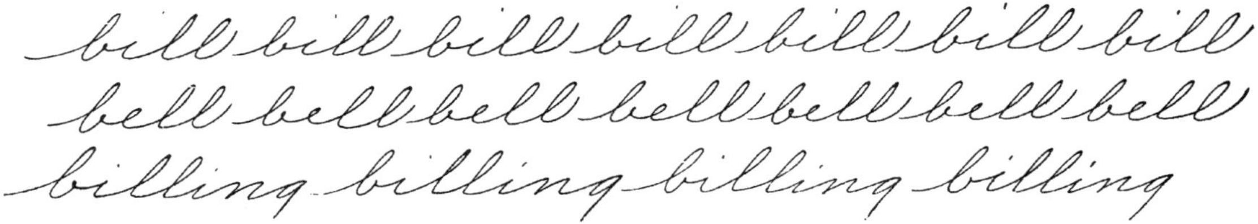

Students are expected to practice the above words as movement drills. The speed in the first two lines of copy should be from twenty-five to thirty words to the minute. At this rate of speed, form can be improved while movement is being developed. The word billing may be practiced at from twelve to fourteen a minute.

LESSON 61

DRILL 98

As an opening movement drill, practice the interlaced oval as shown in the second part of drill 3, lesson 6, and follow with the small **o, m** and n drills in number 19, lesson 16.

Study the enlarged form before attempting the drill. Make fourteen sets of four each or fifty-six small k's to the minute. Keep the letters down to the size of the copies.

LESSON 62

Review lesson 61.

DRILL 99.

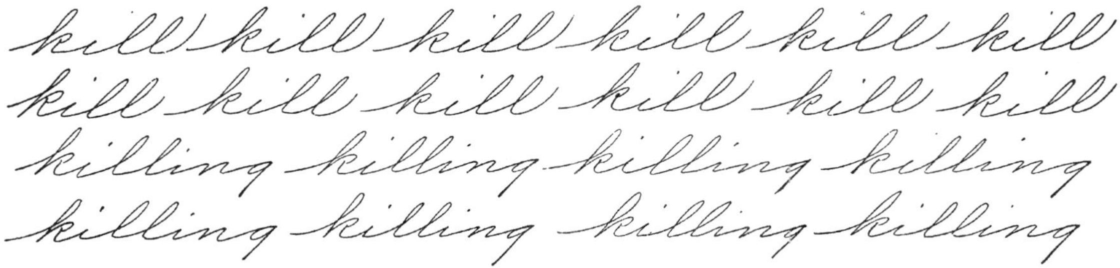

These copies were engraved the same size as written, and we think this writing large enough. Students should make frequent comparisons of size. These copies were written at the following rate of speed, the word kill, twenty-two words, and the work killing, fifteen words to the minute. This is a fair practice speed, but not too fast.

LESSON 63

Practice the compact oval drill 7, lesson 8, five minutes, and imitate the printed copy as closely as possible in size and form. Carry the pen as lightly as possible, and make no less than 150 downward strokes to the minute.

TO RELIEVE MUSCULAR TENSION

It is often an advantage to go over the path of the letters or exercises with the pen in the air. This method is especially helpful to a student whose muscles are hard and who finds difficulty in overcoming the tendency to keep the muscles of the arm and body in a rigid condition. This plan has been suggested in former lessons, and we consider it of sufficient importance to receive emphasis here.

Another plan which the author has recently found helpful to students who write with strained muscles, is to place a paper weight on the paper, and write with the left arm hanging at the side. Under this plan the tension on the right arm is relieved at once.

Still another plan to relieve this tension so common among beginners, is to select some easy drill like small o or m, and make it across the lines of the paper while keeping the eyes fixed upon some object at a distance and on a level with the eyes when the body is fairly erect.

Drill 100

The small f is a little shorter below than above the base line, and the lower point joins with the main downward stroke one-half space above the base line. A fair rate of practice speed is sixteen groups of five letters each, or eighty letters to the minute.

LESSON 64

Review lesson 63.

Drill 101

Write several lines of the word full before changing to the word fill.

LESSON 65

Review lessons 63 and 64.

DRILL 102

Constant repetition is a necessary concomitant in chirographic success.

F fulfill fulfill fulfill full
fulfill fulfill fulfill fulfill
fulfill fulfill fulfill fulfill

All copies in these lessons were written rapidly; with an easy motion.

Rate of practice speed, fifteen or sixteen of the words fulfill, falling and filling to the minute. Good movement leads to good writing; good position leads to good movement. Watch the position; watch the movement.

LESSON 66

Let us emphasize the statement made in a preceding lesson, that constant repetition is neccessary in developing a good style of writing for business. Another thing for the student to bear in mind, is the fact that the only way to learn to execute business writing is to practice business writing. Review lessons 2, 6, 7, 8 and 9, omitting drill 7 in lesson 8.

LESSON 67

DRILL 103

D D D D Deee Deee Deee
D D D D D D D D D D D D
Drumming Drumming Drumming

Compare the oval of the capital D with the capital O. Do not neglect to make a careful study of the D; first each part by itself, and then the letter as a whole. Do not drag the hand over the paper, but keep the writing hand well up in front of the eyes and drive it along firmly, but lightly. It takes a little time, energy and enthusiastic practice to make a good business writer, but it is encouraging to know that under the muscular movement plan there are no failures, when favorable conditions prevail. Practice the capital D until you can make from fifty-five to sixty-five fairly good letters to the minute.

In writing the word Drumming, do not lift the pen from the beginning stroke in small r to the ending stroke of small g. Regularity and continuity of motion are very essential. Keep the pen on the paper. The word Drumming should be practiced at a rate of ten to a minute.

LESSON 68

Drill 104

Drill 105

Above are given two styles of capital T. In these lessons the author has, in very few cases, presented more than one style of capital, but in capitals F and T there seems to be much divergence of opinion among successful teachers of business writing regarding the best form to adopt, and we have thought it best to give the student an opportunity of making a selection. Of course, a simple cross stroke will change any of the foregoing forms into a capital F.

For capital T, the author does not especially favor either of the forms above given, but prefers the following :

Drill 106

Do not make the beginning part too high; it should be but little more than two-thirds the entire height of the letter. Note particularly that the last part curves over the top of the main (first) part without touching it. Time and hard work will be important factors in developing this letter. Be earnest, be faithful. The count is 1, 2, 3, 4, and about forty-five letters should be made to the minute.

Drill 107

Write five words to a foolscap line.

LESSON 69

DRILL 108

In twelve of the business capitals we have the fish hook or small loop beginning. Most pupils find this style of starting the capital letters here given somewhat difficult at first, but when fully mastered it becomes a favorite. It is of sufficient importance to be given considerable study and practice.

The first copy shows the fish hook beginning, and in execution compels a checking of the movement at the top at the union of the strokes. In using the small loop, no checking of the motion is necessary.

A careful study and comparison of these capitals will show that in F, Q, W, X and Z the main downward strokes are curved much more than in H, K, M and N, while in U, V and Y compound curves are used in these main strokes.

Practice the first two parts at the left of the line. The completed capitals are mainly for study.

DRILL 109

Capital Q, as shown above, is simply the enlarged form of figure 2. Curve the main downward stroke liberally. Make the lower loop flat on the base line and drop the finishing curve below. Students should frequently compare their writing with the copies.

The mind directs, the arm and hand perform, and both mind and muscle must work in harmony.

No matter how perfectly the muscles of the arm are trained, good letters cannot be made unless a good conception of form is in the mind. Capital Q should be made well at from sixty to seventy to the minute and the figure 2 faster. The count in each case 1, 2, 3.

DRILL 110

The following small g drill is in the line of repetition. Much is to be gained by frequent reviews of familiar drills.

DRILL 111

In the style of writing here presented the loop of small g extends three spaces below the base line. The paper should be held in such a position that the downward strokes are pulled toward a point central between the eyes, the paper being changed from time to time with the left hand to keep its position relatively the same. The motion should be purely muscular throughout, and the movement in making the loop particularly quick and elastic. Study the form closely and note the crossing of the loop with a left curve on the base.

In groups of four connected letters, a speed of sixty-four letters to the minute should be attained. A count of eight for each group of four will aid in regulating the movement.

DRILL 112

By comparison it will be seen that the q is a little shorter below the base than the g; that the turn at the bottom is made to the right instead of the left and that the lower part connects on the base line with the first part. On account of the check given the motion at the connective point a less number of letters are made to the minute than in small g, but the movement should be quick.

LESSON 70

DRILL 113

The inverted small e preceding the capital K will not only aid in developing the small loop beginning, but will force freedom of movement and lightness of stroke.

Count 1, 2, 3, 4 for the drill and first part of the capital H, and count 1, 2 for the last part. In making the last part swing the hand in the same manner and direction as for the beginning stroke of capital O, but straighten the stroke from its center to base. Let nothing escape you; observe closely every stroke, no matter how minute or unimportant it may appear.

DRILL 114

With an easy, swinging movement make from thirty-five to forty capitals of above form to the minute in a count of 1, 2, 3, 4.

The beginning loop may be made smaller than in the copy, but no larger in business writing.

The capital K is a natural companion to the capital H. The beginning strokes in both letters are identical in size and shape.

Drill 115

Careful study of the last part of the K will be very much to the advantage of every student. Cover the first part of the letter with a piece of paper and then study the last part. Turn the copy upside down and study it in that position. Notice particularly that the loop in the last part grasps the first part a little above the center.

LESSON 71

Drill 116

Forty capitals of the above form to the minute will be a fair rate of speed. Compare your capitals frequently with the copy.

Drill 117

This is a most excellent word to practice at this stage of the work. It is a good movement developer. Give close attention to size, general appearance and the spaces between letters and guard against irregular movement. Keep the hand well up in front of the eyes and drive the pen over the paper lightly. Write a half page of the copy and then make a careful study of your work. Try to write each line better than the one preceding it. Usually four words of this copy should be written to the line.

LESSON 72

Drill 118

Another helpful movement drill. See how closely you can imitate the copy.

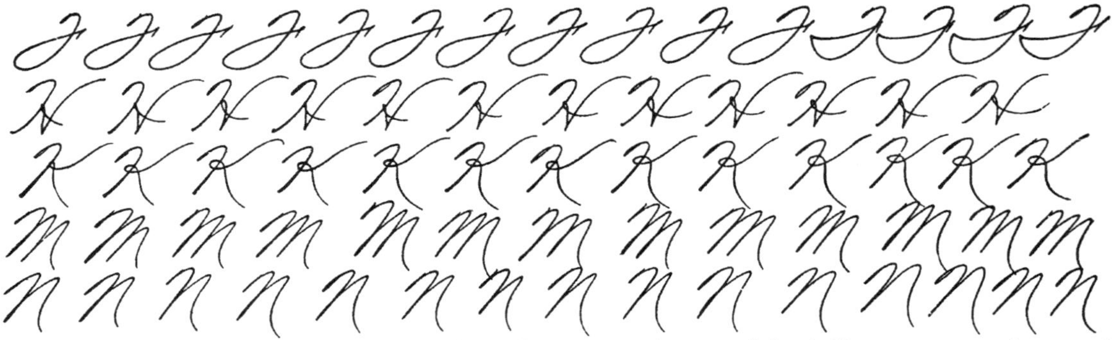

Work faithfully on every letter. Repeat the form of each letter over and over until decided improvement can be seen. Make frequent comparisons. Study length, breadth, curves and connections closely.

Rate of practice speed to the minute, F, sixty; H, thirty-five to forty; M, forty-five to fifty-five; N, sixty.

LESSON 73

DRILL 120

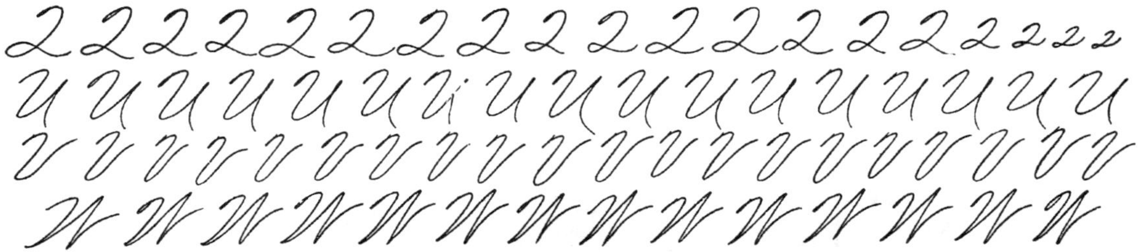

Rate of practice speed, Q, thirty-seven; U, fifty-fix; V, sixty-eight; W, 44 to the minute.

POINTS TO OBSERVE—Capital Q is the enlarged form of the figure 2. The last parts of capitals U, V, and W are shorter than the other parts and the first main strokes in U and V are exactly alike. In making capital W, check the motion a little at the base line in the first main downward stroke, as this will aid in the construction of the first part.

LESSON 74

DRILL 121

A Compact Oval by H. S. Spencer, Student

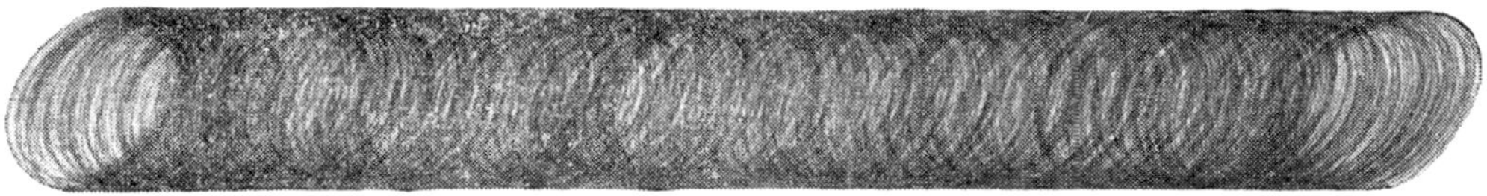

DRILL 122

Study and compare as you practice. Drill speed to the minute on these capitals: X, 48; Y, 48; Z, 56.

REVIEW WORK

At this point it would be a good plan to review all of the essential work of the preceding lessons. From one to two weeks should be spent in such practice.

LESSON 75

DRILL 123

In the letters j and z in drill 123 are given two small letters not found in any of the preceding lessons. Some authors make the loops of the j and z shorter below the base than small y and g, but we make no distinction. The upper part of j is the small i. Small z should receive careful attention.

LESSON 76

ABOUT SIZE

In these lessons we are presenting a style of writing that can be easily and rapidly executed, and that while large enough to be perfectly legible, is small enough for general use. Examine the writing of the best business writers in the large mercantile centers and it will be seen that the writing here presented is large enough.

It is, in our judgment, a grave error to present models from which pupils are to practice that are larger than the students will be expected to write when they enter the employ of business firms, and yet many professional penmen continue to present to their students in business writing, models that are not only two or three times larger than good business writing is expected to be, but that abound in forms that cannot possibly be executed at a high rate of speed.

CAPITAL AND WORD PRACTICE AS MOVEMENT DRILLS

In some of the following copies we present capital and word practice that is intended to encourage free movement, continuity in execution, and a better control of the writing muscles than has, perhaps, been gained up to this point. The plan is to repeat the capital until it can be made at the rate of speed designated, and to follow with the word practice. In the word drills, the value of a continuous movement must not be lost sight of, and the pen should remain on the paper from the beginning to the ending of the small letters. In fact all of the copies should be treated as movement drills. Words ending in ing have been purposely selected and their value in the plan of development will not be questioned, if they are rightly practiced.

DRILL 124

The rate of speed for capital A is from seventy-five to eighty-five good letters to the minute. Practice speed for the word Alling, about fifteen a minute.

LESSON 77

No other opening movement drill than the capital C itself is necessary in starting this lesson. Eighty to the minute is a good practice speed.

DRILL 125

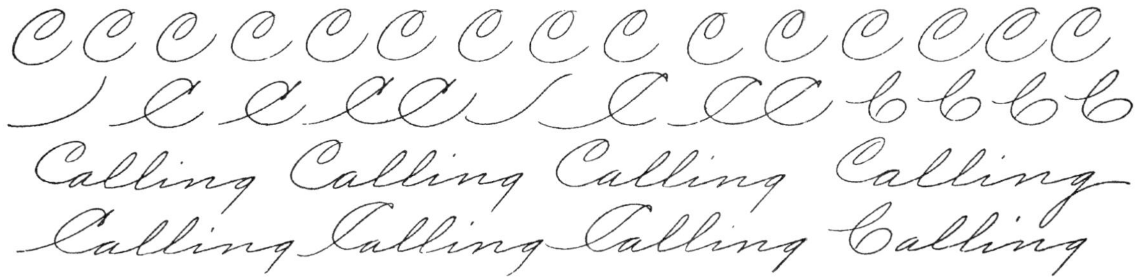

Practice the word Calling at sixteen or more to the minute.

LESSON 78

DRILL 126

Open the lesson with a drill on the capital O as in the copy above given, making fully seventy to the minute, and write the word Oiling at the rate of fourteen to the minute. Watch position; watch movement.

LESSON 79

DRILL 127

The capital L, rightly practiced, is an excellent movement drill at this stage of the work.

Questions you should be able to answer intelligently: Where and how does the beginning stroke start? How long is the upper loop, compared to the length of the letter? Is the downward stroke a straight line or a curve? Is the lower loop round or flat and what part rests on the base line? Is the final stroke finished on or below the base line?

Compare your work with the copy in reference to these questions. Practice speed, sixty or seventy letters to the minute. Write the word Lanning with a very light motion at not less than sixteen to the minute.

LESSON 80

DRILL 128

Do not overlook the proportion of the capital M as illustrated and explained in lesson 21, drill 26. Practice speed of the M, about forty to the minute, and the word Milling, fourteen words in a minute, and a higher rate of speed for some students.

LESSON 81

SPECIAL NOTICE—Students who cannot use and apply the muscular movement with fair accuracy should return to and review the beginning lessons, studying carefully all the instructions regarding position, penholding and methods of developing movement.

DRILL 129

Capital N should be made at the rate of fifty-five or sixty per minute. Practice speed for Nulling, twelve to sixteen to the minute.

LESSON 82

DRILL 130

The capital H should be made at the rate of thirty-five or forty per minute, and the word Hauling about fifteen to the minute.

LESSON 83

Forty capital K's to the minute is a fair rate of speed. Students should not lose sight of the fact that the motion determines the form. Take care of the motion and the form of the letters will develop easily and naturally. A careful study of the movement as applied to the capital K will be helpful. After making the first part of the letter, the hand (with the pen in the air) should swing below the base line, describing an oval and returning upward and to the left to the beginning point of the last part of the letter. Be sure to connect the last with the first part with a loop, as shown in the copy. Drop the finishing part below the base line.

About twelve of the words should be made to the minute.

DRILL 131

LESSON 84

DRILL 132

Practice the capital P at the rate of from fifty to sixty letters to the minute. The word Pulling should be written at the rate of twelve words per minute. Some pupils will be able to write the word at a higher rate of speed and still do good work.

LESSON 85

Be sure to fix in the mind the image of the letter before attempting to make it. Study closely the proportions and the direction of every stroke. Make about fifty capital R's to the minute.

Do not forget that your advancement depends upon movement, and that movement depends upon position. The body should be self-supporting, with the feet squarely on the floor. The body should not crowd against the desk; the right arm should be well out from the side; the right hand should be well in front of the eyes, and the paper should be from twelve to fourteen inches from the eyes.

If the wrist or side of the hand rests on the paper, all motion coming from the muscles of the arm will stop at the wrist and it will be an impossibility to use the muscular movement. Watch the wrist and the side of the hand closely. Remember that the propelling power is located above the elbow, in the upper arm and shoulder.

Write line after line of the word Running with a light, quick motion, and compare your writing with the copy frequently.

DRILL 133

LESSON 86

DRILL 134

Turn to lesson 43, and practice and study capital S in accordance with the instructions given in that lesson. Enough time should be reserved to write at least one foolscap page of the word Swelling.

LESSON 87

DRILL 135

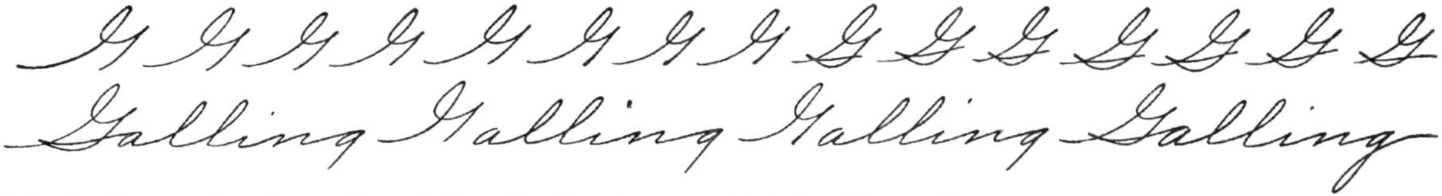

Students who cannot make good loop letters should make a special study of lesson 27.

LESSON 88

DRILL 136

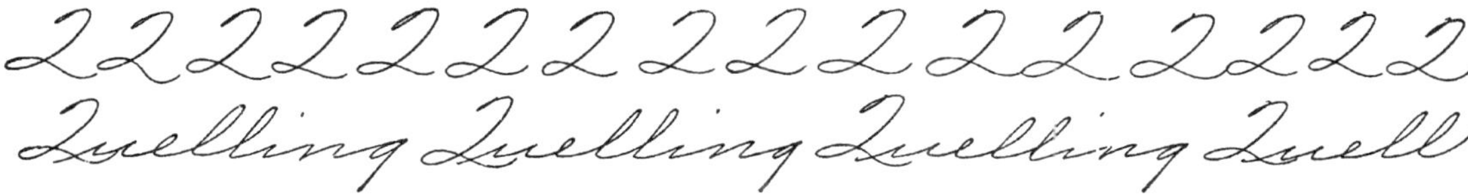

As explained in a former lesson, the capital Q is nothing more than a large figure 2. It is a good movement drill. Practice it as such. In all your word practice a special effort should be made to space the letters evenly. Study your written lines with that in mind.

LESSON 89

Students should give particular attention to the appearance of their finished pages, making the letters and words conform to the spaces they occupy. The capitals given in these lessons should occupy only from two-thirds to three-fourths the distance between ruled lines, assuming that such lines are about three-eighths of an inch apart.

From eighteen to twenty capitals should be made to a line. If the forms are fairly well made, a page of capitals written in accordance with above suggestions will present an appearance that will be very pleasing to most business men.

The crossing of the capital F is above the center of the letter, and the final stroke at the crossing is small. In the word practice write the full word every time the capital is made. Do not let your practice work approach scribbling. Do the very best you can, not part of the time, but *all* the time.

Drill 137

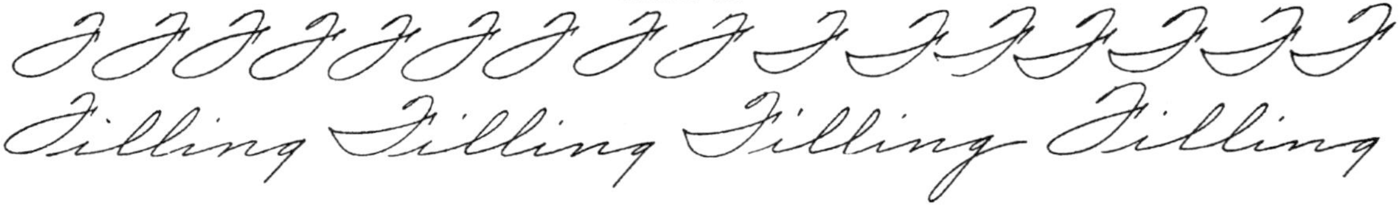

LESSON 90

Drill 138

Always start the capital I with an upward stroke from below the base line. The upper part should be about one-half the width of the lower. The crossing of the main upward with the main downward stroke should be one space above the base line. Practice the detached capital as well as the word until there is an improvement in the movement and its application.

LESSON 91

Drill 139

Practice and compare, and then practice again. Capital J is twice as wide above as below the base, and the lower part is a little shorter than the upper part. Students who find the letter troublesome should review lesson 38.

LESSON 92

DRILL 140

Write a page of capital E's and another of the word Elling.

LESSON 93

DRILL 141

Capital B was discussed at considerable length in lesson 57, and students who have failed to master the letter should turn to and review that lesson.

LESSON 94

DRILL 142

Students should make their letters no larger than the copies. Write line after line of the detached capital before writing the word. Rate of speed for practice, fifty to fifty-five capitals and fourteen words in a minute.

LESSON 95

Drill 143

The first part of capital T should be no more than half the entire height of the letter. Give attention to the abrupt stop on the base line in the first part of the letter. Carry the last part up and clear over the first part in a graceful curve. Practice the word as well as the detached capital.

LESSON 96

Drill 144

Capital W should be very closely studied. The tendency is to slant the last part too much, tipping it away from the first part. The first upward stroke is a right curve, and the construction of the last part and the appearance of the entire letter are to a considerable extent dependent upon that line.

In making the first part there should be a stop at the base line. This will aid very much in the construction of the last part of the letter. The last line in the letter, it will be noticed, is shorter than the two center strokes. It is unlikely that students who fail to study its construction closely will learn to make a good capital W. The rate of practice speed should be between forty and fifty letters to a minute. Do not neglect the word practice.

LESSON 97

The last part of the capital U is shorter than the first part. Study the letter until you have a good mental picture of it. Make the U at the rate of forty-five to a minute, and do not neglect the word practice.

DRILL 145

LESSON 98

DRILL 146

An otherwise good capital V will be spoiled if the finishing line is too long. Notice its length. Study and practice should go hand in hand. Do not neglect either.

LESSON 99

DRILL 147

Rifle practice Shoot straight

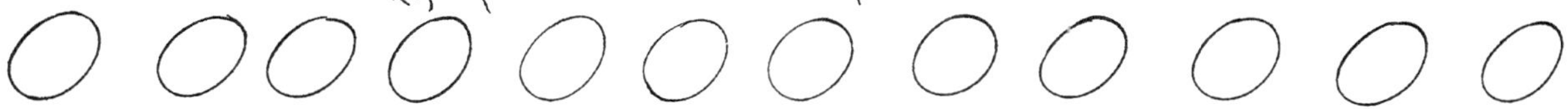

The above drill is a good test movement. The lines must be sharp and firm throughout, and it must be evident that to produce such lines the pen must move rapidly. Gain momentum by making the form once with the pen in the air, and without checking the motion bring the pen to the paper on the second downward stroke. Time is wasted in practicing this or any other drill given in these lessons with a slow, halting movement.

CAUTION TO TEACHERS AND PUPILS

The development of good business writing is dependent, first, upon proper clothing of the writing arm; second, upon a substantial desk or table of the right height; third, upon a good position at the desk; fourth, upon a relaxed condition of the writing muscles; fifth, upon the freedom of the wrist and the side of the hand from the paper; and sixth, upon concentration, determination, and constantly repeated effort. Teachers who cannot maintain enthusiasm throughout the writing period, and who cannot become resigned to the necessity of constantly repeated cautions and admonitions along the lines above indicated, must never expect to meet with flattering results.

Teachers, see that your pupils are alert, watchful, and in their penmanship practice constantly working under the most favorable conditions. Force upon the inner consciousness of every pupil the harmfulness of careless practice, and the necessity of making every stroke count in the right direction.

Students, do not vehemently assert that you are very anxious to become good writers and then abuse the opportunities that are within your reach. Learning to write well is not difficult to the earnest, careful, hardworking pupil, and with such results almost immediately follow correct methods of practice.

Finger and muscular movements are antagonistic, and the student who makes an effort to use muscular movement in the writing class need hope for but little success.

Home students, those not having the advantage of the directing council of good teachers, should frequently review the beginning lessons.

DRILL 148

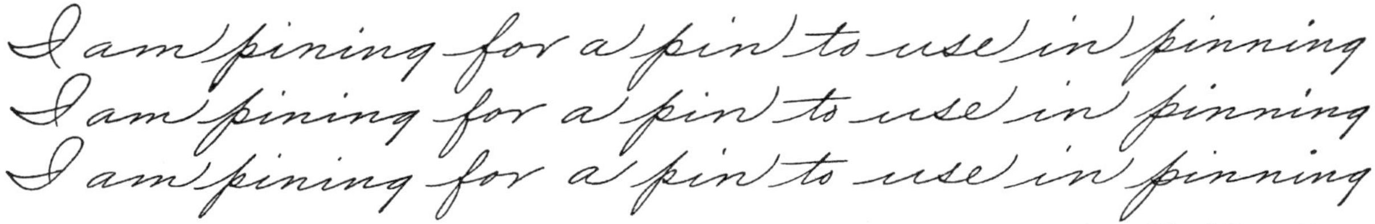

First, practice the above copy in sections. Repeat the capital I until the form is good when made rapidly, follow with several lines of the word am, and so continue to practice each word in the copy until uniformity in spacing, height and slant have been developed. Then write a page of the complete copy and criticise it.

As simple as it looks, there is material for several hours' practice in this copy.

LESSON 100

DRILL 149

Drill **149** looks like ornamental writing, does it not? No matter if it does, it is an excellent movement drill at this stage of the **work.** **It is what we term a forcing drill, and those who practice it will soon discover that it will disclose any weakness in movement. After the form has been fairly well mastered, about seventy connected letters should be made to a minute. In regulating class speed a count of three may be used.**

DRILL 150

Amos B. Collins owns the mill on the hill
Amos B. Collins owns the mill on the hill
Amos B. Collins owns the mill on the hill

The same method of practice should be followed in this copy as in number 148.

LESSON 101

Open this lesson with a short drill on number 149 and follow with small o, m and n, just three or four lines of each.

DRILL 151

Specimens of my business penmanship
Specimens of my business penmanship
Specimens of my business penmanship.

First practice number 151 word by word before writing a complete line. Follow with a full page of the completed copy, and do not neglect to criticise the results. Height, spacing and slant should receive especial attention.

LESSON 102

DRILL 152

Here is another drill, the specific object of which is to force movement. There are no straight lines in this copy; all are curves. Note that fact and also that the flourish, the superfluous line, covers more space than the letter itself. No progress can be made with this letter unless a light, firm and quick movement is used. The flourished O drill and the connected capital A exercise may frequently and very profitably take the place of the compact oval drills given in the beginning lessons. In practicing No. 152 an excessively rapid motion is not necessary, and, in fact, will prove harmful, but, on the other hand, the motion must not drag. Fifty good letters in a minute is a fair practice rate of speed.

LINE AND PAGE PRACTICE

In several lessons following, are given copies in line writing from which pages should be written. It may be a comparatively easy matter for some students to write one or two lines in an attractive manner, who cannot maintain the same degree of excellence throughout a page. The special object sought in this work should be the writing of attractive pages at a commercial rate of speed. To attain this end, students should study the appearance of the finished line and page from time to time, and always try to harmonize the writing with the place it occupies.

Some of the lines are peculiar as viewed from a standpoint of composition, but they have been constructed to embrace a repetition of small letters that usually require a great deal of practice.

DRILL 153

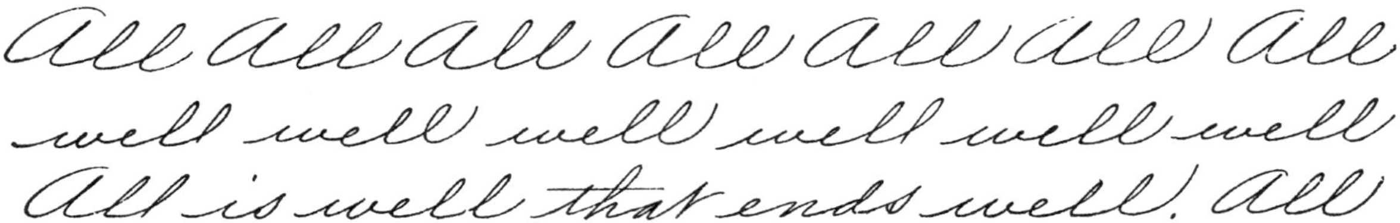

Practice this copy as given. Write the word All, over and over, until the motion used is almost automatic and until a marked improvement is shown in the general appearance. Practice the word well, in the same manner. Write the lower line at the rate of four or five lines to the minute. Keep this up for fully ten minutes without stopping a second, except to take ink, and some of the kinks will be taken out of the arms.

LESSON 103

Drill 154

Bill was billing bluing and blacking

Do not rest a moment until you have filled one page with above copy; then examine the appearance of the page as a whole. Do not write larger than the copy.

LESSON 104

Drill 155

Dutiful daughters do devious duties.

Make a few lines of capital D's before writing the line.

Do not lose sight of the fact that position at the desk has much to do with the development of the writing. Position refers to feet, chair, body, arms, wrist, fingers, pen, head and paper. In preceding lessons enough has been said about these things to make extended instructions here unnecessary.

LESSON 105

Drill 156

Faithfully fulfill all promises. F.

Uniform slant is hard to maintain in this copy. After writing a few lines pick out the faults and endeavor to correct them.

LESSON 106

Drill 157

Gaming is a galling, gulling pastime.

Above is the copy of this lesson for practice. Solid pages are wanted and not haphazard practice.

LESSON 107

Drill 158

Hold happiness more sacred than gold

Practice the capital H as a movement drill a few minutes before working on the copy given above. Maintain equal distances, not only between letters, but between words as well.

LESSON 108

Drill 159

Jolly judges judging jumping jokers

LESSON 109

Drill 160

Kick the kinks out of the kicking colt

It may be best to spend some time on special practice of small k.

LESSON 110

DRILL 161

L Lulling breezes whispering slumber.

Move the pen lightly, quickly and continuously.

LESSON 111

DRILL 162

Mills and Milligan are millers Mmmm

DRILL 163

Nine months after date I promise to pay

LESSON 112

DRILL 164

One by one the sands are flowing One.

Practice the capital O as a movement drill a few minutes and then do your best on the entire copy.

LESSON 113

DRILL 165

Pulling, pushing, popular populace.

LESSON 114

DRILL 166

Quimby was quick to quash a quibble

This copy is not easy. It is difficult enough to merit careful practice for a full writing period. It will be best to practice the capital Q as a movement drill before writing the entire lesson.

LESSON 115

DRILL 167

Rolling muscular movement is the best.

LESSON 116

DRILL 168

Summer sunshine follows spring.

LESSON 117

DRILL 169

Time and tide wait for no man.

LESSON 118

DRILL 170

Important improvement in penmanship

LESSON 119

DRILL 171

Union of interests brings union of minds.

It is always a good plan, where time permits, to first practice each capital at the beginning of the line as a repeated drill.

LESSON 120

DRILL 172

Value your time as you value money

Do not neglect the movement drills because they are not specially mentioned in every lesson.

LESSON 121

DRILL 173

Willing William was willing to watch.

Do not practice both styles of capital W. Select the style you prefer and stick to it.

LESSON 122

DRILL 174

Xenophon fixed historical events.

The capital X is made with a figure six inverted, and a figure six right side up. Keep this idea in mind when making it.

LESSON 123

Drill 175

Young men, grasp your opportunity.

LESSON 124

Drill 176

Zero weather gives zest to pedestrians.

LESSON 125

Drill 177

Pay James C. Robins on demand One

LESSON 126

Drill 178

Due E. F. Gilman Nine Hundred
Due E. F. Gilman Nine Hundred
Due E. F. Gilman Nine Hundred

Work up to the complete copy by systematic practice on the capitals and words.

LESSON 127

DRILL 179

The author, in common with many teachers of business writing, has found the practice of combinations of capitals in his classes very helpful in developing accuracy and freedom. This is an excellent part of the course in which to introduce such drills, but tangled and difficult combinations should be avoided.

Drill 179, if rightly practiced, will force light movement and develop constructive ability. About twenty-two of the combination C P R should be made to a minute.

DRILL 180

A few scattered lines of copy 180 will not meet the requirements. Write a full page.

LESSON 128

DRILL 181

Practice the combination of capitals several minutes before practicing the small letters. A perfect mastery of this combination will help students in the work that will follow.

LESSON 129

DRILL 182

Use a uniform motion from beginning to end in this combination, and make about twenty-five in a minute.

Drill 183

LESSON 130

Drill 184

Number 184 affords a good drill and a good test of accuracy in applying movement. The last downward stroke in the capital H is a left curve, is it not? Study the direction of the pen in making it, and then strike off boldly. This will be a good drill to practice frequently at the beginning of a lesson.

Drill 185

Use your eyes; focus your mind upon the work, study and practice earnestly, and you will be pleased with the results.

LESSON 131

Movement drills for a few minutes and then the following:

Drill 186

Practice the combinations of capitals several minutes before making the small letters. Such repeated effort will be helpful.

LESSON 132

Drill 187

After vigorous oval drills the student will be ready for 186. Repeat the combinations of capitals over and over until uniformity in size, shape, and slant can be maintained.

LESSON 133

DRILL 188

Pure muscular movement is expected. Do not permit the fingers holding the pen to extend or contract. Make about twenty-one of these combinations to a minute.

DRILL 189

Write a full page of this copy if time permits. Make frequent comparisons and criticisms.

LESSON 134

DRILL 190

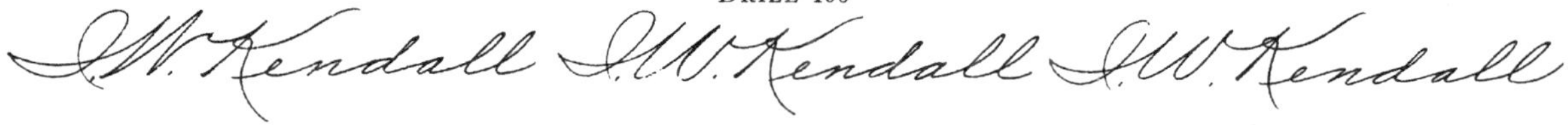

LESSON 135

DRILL 191

LESSON 136

DRILL 192

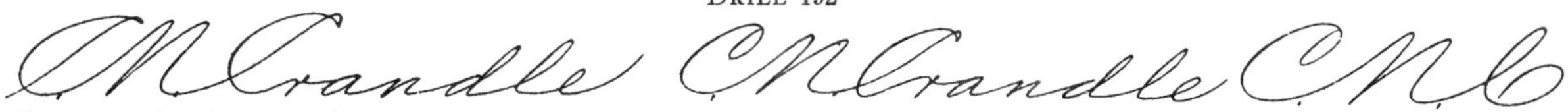

Slight variations in styles of capitals are given in number 191. Students may select one style and practice that only, and the same plan should be followed in the following copy.

Drill 193

A. C. Grimes A. C. Grimes. A. C. G

LESSON 137

Drill 194

C. A. Faust C. A. Faust C. A. F

LESSON 138

Drill 195

Z. N. U. Z. N. Upton Z. N. Upton Z. N. Upton

LESSON 139

Drill 196

X. S. Hammond X. S. Hammond X. S. H

LESSON 140

Drill 197

V. W. Young V. W. Young W. V. Young

VARIETY OF BUSINESS WRITING AND BUSINESS FORMS

It is the argument of the author of the Palmer Method of Business Writing that students who follow the lessons to a successful completion have left to them the possibility of individuality in their future writing.

In nearly all capitals there are several good business forms, either one of which may be adopted and successfully used by one who has mastered the Muscular Movement. It is not best, however, that students should adopt for final use, several styles of any capital, but the better plan is for students as they complete the final lessons in the Palmer Method to select a plain business form of each capital and permanently adopt it. Such a form may be found in the penmanship of some good business writer whose work is not represented in this book, and it may be found on a stray bit of paper.

It is a fact, however, that the majority of those who learned the Palmer Method ten or more years ago under the individual instruction of the author, or through his printed lessons, and have since been employed in offices, have found the general style of writing under this method well adapted to business uses and have retained it with practically no modifications.

In the following specimens of business writing we have made selections from different teachers of penmanship, and good business writers that conform to the general plan of the preceding lessons and that furnish good copies from which advanced students may practice.

E. O. Folsom,
Sheboygan, Wis. June 15, 1901.
Palmer Method of Business Writing
I use and advocate the Muscular
Movement System of Penmanship.
I write rapidly; I write easily; and
I can write hour after hour without
getting tired.

It was more than ten years ago that Mr. Folsom finished his business course which included a course in business writing. He is a teacher.

Waterloo, Iowa, June 8, 1901.

The Palmer Method of Business Writing.
I use and advocate the Muscu-
lar Movement System of Penmanship
I write easily, I write rapidly,
and I can write hour after hour with-
out getting tired.

Very truly
E. A. Boggs.

Mr. E. A. Boggs finished his penmanship practice ten years ago and is now a bookkeeper.

Business Capitals by C. C. Lister, Sadler's Business College, Baltimore, Md.

George Heineman,

Sommerville, Ind.

Dear Sir,—Your favor of the 6th instant received. We should be pleased to meet your Mr. James King, and if his statement is approved we shall be happy to grant you the credit named, and serve you as satisfactorily as we have heretofore endeavored to in our cash transactions.

We remain

Very truly yours,

Farrington, Davis & Co.

By H. B. Lehman, Cleveland, Ohio.

Friend Palmer,

The Federation issue of "The Western Penman" is received. In my opinion it is the handsomest number you have ever published. Success to you

Sincerely

L. Madarász.

By L. Madarasz, New York City.

Friend Palmer,

Believing in a simple rapid system of business writing, and recognizing in the Western Penman an able exponent of my creed. I take pleasure in enclosing New York exchange for fifty-six suscriptions.

Yours truly,

C. E. Doner.

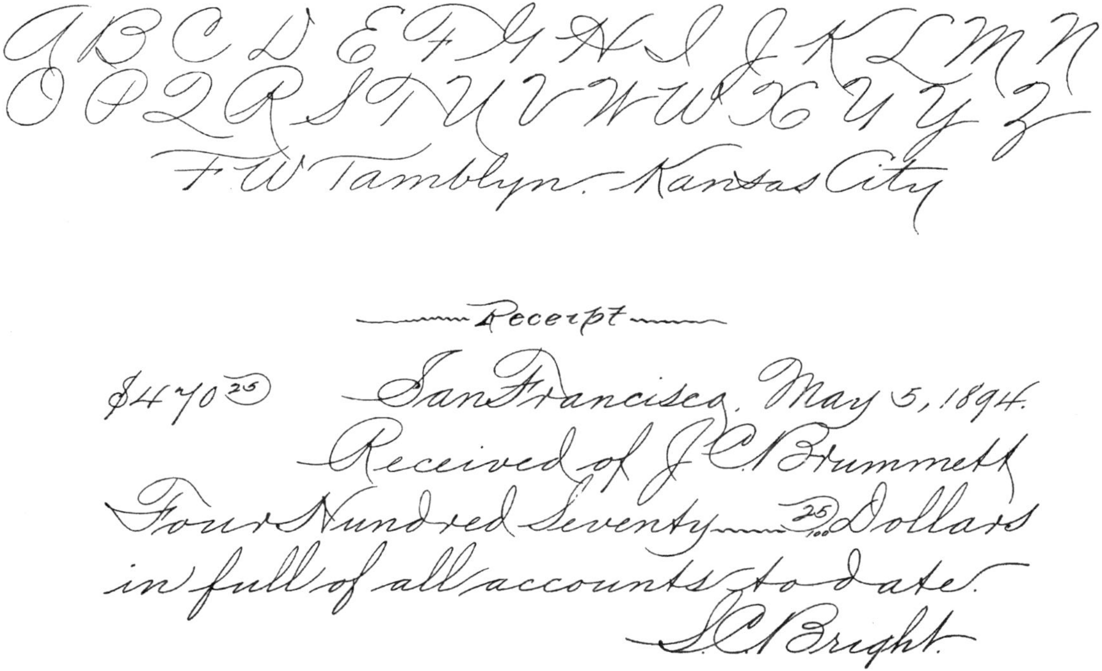

By F. W. Tamblyn, Kansas City, Mo.

Jan. Feb. Mar. Apr. May June

July Aug. Sept. Oct. Nov. Dec.

$888# Ellenville, N.Y., Apr. 10, 1901.

At thirty days sight pay to

Emerson E. Eastwood —————— or Order,

Eight Hundred and Eighty-eight # Dollars,

value received and charge to the account of

To E. E. Eaton, Emmons Ernest & Co

Elgin, Ill.

Business Writing by W. C. Henning, Cedar Rapids, Iowa.

St Louis, Mo., June 1, 1901.

Mr. A. N. Palmer, Editor,
The Western Penman,
Cedar Rapids, Ia.

My dear Sir, — This is submitted as a specimen of my business penmanship written with a free muscular movement at a commercial rate of speed. While it may not be so accurate as some would like, it meets every requirement of business, and the possessor of a similar style of writing can always find a market for his services.

Respectfully

By W. C. Henning, Cedar Rapids, Iowa.

$777.00 Sing Sing, Sept. 7, 1900.

Received of Samuel S. Stevens & Sons, Seven Hundred and Seventy-seven Dollars, in full of account to date

S. S. Simmons, Sr.

Mr A. N. Palmer, Prest,
The Western Penman Pub Co,
Cedar Rapids, Iowa.
Dear Sir,-

C. W. Dumanois, Esq.,
Davison, Mich
Dear Sir,-

Courtney, Amburn & Co.,
Galveston, Texas.
Gentlemen,-

By W. C. Henning, Cedar Rapids, Iowa.

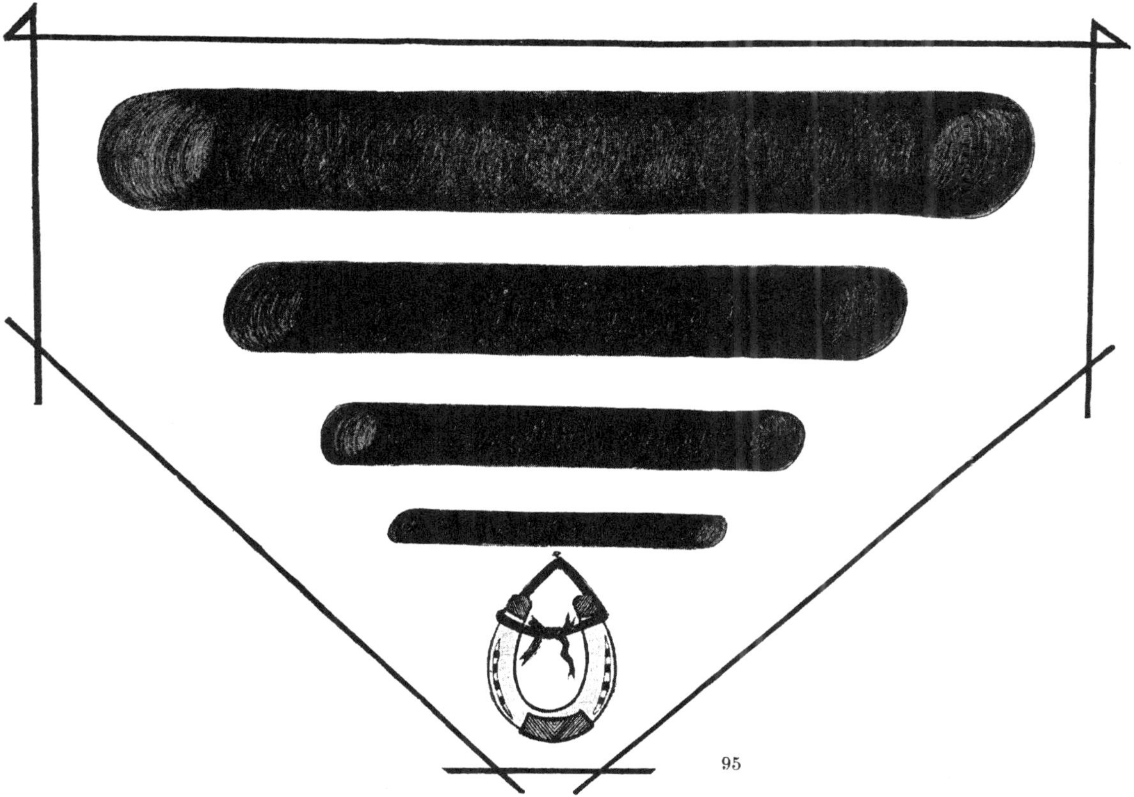

St Mary's Academy
Monroe, Mich. Jan. 18. 1901.
This is a Specimen of my business writing.
This is a specimen of my business writing
This is a specimen of my business writing
Mary E. Dunigan.

St Mary's Academy,
Monroe, Mich. April 20, 1901.
Palmer Method of Penmanship.
A plain specimen of my
business penmanship.
Mary Dunigan.

These specimens show how great an improvement may be made in penmanship in three months by an earnest pupil who follows the Palmer Method.